DATE DUE

MR 11 '94			
OC 28 '94			
DE 9 '94			
NO 11 00			
AP 25 02			

Demco, Inc. 38-293

THE
END
OF THE
COLD
WAR

THE
END
OF THE
COLD
WAR

European Unity,
Socialism, and the
Shift in Global Power

∎

Bogdan Denitch

∎

University of Minnesota Press
MINNEAPOLIS

Published by the University of Minnesota Press
2037 University Avenue Southeast, Minneapolis, MN 55414.
Printed in the United States of America.

Library of Congress Cataloging-in-Publication Data

Denitch, Bogdan Denis.
    The end of the Cold War : European unity, socialism, and the shift
in global power / Bogdan Denitch.
        p.   cm.
    Includes bibliographical references.
    ISBN 0–8166–1872–0. — ISBN 0–8166–1875–5 (pbk.)
    1. Europe—Politics and government—1945-   2. Cold War.
    I. Title.
    D1053.D46   1990
    940.55—dc20   90–10873
                                                                   CIP

To Michael Harrington (1928–1989)

*Companion, friend, and comrade
for forty years*

Contents

Preface

The End of the Cold War
Background and Consequences

The three developments that will dominate the international political scene for the remainder of the twentieth century are the end of the cold war between the alliances led by the United States and the Soviet Union; European unification, which will expand the European "space" from the European Economic Community (EEC) to the European Fair Trade Association (EFTA), with Eastern Europe and the Soviet Union increasingly sharing in the "common European home"; and the democratic upheavals and reforms in Eastern Europe and the Soviet Union, which mark the end of the communist dictatorships. Each of these developments will have massive consequences, and together they are transforming the world order as we have known it since the end of World War II. Not the least of the consequences will be the decline of both the United States and the Soviet Union in relative significance as the economies of a unified Europe and Japan assume even more importance and as sheer military power decreases in importance. In assessing the three new historical developments that make the 1990s a "hinge" decade in the United States, one needs something that is all too rare in this country, a non-U.S.-centered historical perspective. It is not at all strange that it should be rare, for our schools do not teach history at all seriously. They certainly teach little or nothing, even on a university level, about the Eastern European countries and the Soviet Union, the region in which recent events make these changes possible.

Knowing so little of their past, and therefore inevitably understanding so little either of their present or of their most probable futures, how are we to judge the prospects for democratic reforms in the nations of that region? How are we to evaluate the probable impact of the collapse of the Communist parties and their authoritarian regimes? But we *must* try to understand this development because it has vital bearing on European unification and the end of the cold war. Clearly if the prospects for stable democracies are dim in Eastern Europe and the Soviet Union, then, as some of the old cold warriors are already saying, great instability and insecurity will prevail in the region, and necessarily in Europe as a whole. Economic and political collapse can at least result in massive and uncontrollable immigration, which would jeopardize the prosperous European Community, or at worst give rise to dangerous xenophobic dictatorships based probably on the military. That in turn would put both European unification and the end of the cold war at risk. Much is therefore at stake, and not only for the people of Eastern Europe and the Soviet Union, in the prospects for successful democratic and economic reforms. As far as human rights activists and those who advocate democracy are concerned, it is obviously better to push for help to the processes of democratization with aid now than to wage campaigns against violations of democratic rights later. It is better to help the new democracies now than to protest the dictatorships that will emerge if they fail.

Large-scale aid is needed to help the fledgling democracies. Democratic reforms will have little chance to succeed if the economies remain dismal or, worse, if democracy is associated with social chaos and a general drop in living standards. But for these reforms to flourish it is not enough to remove the repressive hand of the old Communist parties and destroy their political monopoly. It is not even enough to loosen up the economies by introducing some market criteria and release long-suppressed creative political, intellectual, and social energies. What is needed is generous aid, aid on the scale of the Marshall Plan, which helped the Western European democracies rebuild after a devastating war and dictatorship. That help was economic as well as political. To be sure, it was very much in the self-interest of the United States, but nevertheless the aid was real. I argue that assisting the Eastern European and Soviet democratic transformation is in the most direct self-interest of Western democracy. The only problem is that it is not at all clear today which forces in the "West," including the United States, see themselves as having an interest in democracy. That aid is, however, now desperately and urgently needed.

It is tragic to note that the present U.S. administration is doing and will do everything in its power to evade any major financial burden of aid. It is as if the decades of the cold war were forgotten. Can it be that while endless funds were available for armaments, espionage, subsidizing right-wing anticommunist dictators, setting up anticommunist guerrillas, and settling former Nazis and their allies in the United States as well as providing a haven for all, or almost all, who could make a claim to be refugees from communism the United States cannot offer real assistance to the democratic transformations that are bringing communist dictatorships to an end? It seems the answer is yes, there is almost a nostalgia for the certainties of the cold war. Billions of dollars for the cold war, a miserly sum for the genuine victims of decades of communist rule, the peoples of Eastern Europe and the Soviet Union. The Bush administration will generally receive bipartisan support for this stance from the travesty of an opposition party that controls the Congress. This is a consequence of irresponsible fiscal and security policies that have promoted the frittering away of hundreds of billions of dollars for unnecessary armaments but, for the sake of continuing to pay the lowest taxes in the advanced industrial world, cannot find more than a symbolic pittance to help new democratic governments.

More hope lies in aid from Western Europe, from the banks, governments, and even the labor movement. A good deal has already been put on the table, much more than the shameful amount the United States has pledged, but considerably more is needed. In addition to financial aid, help is needed in establishing independent unions, new political parties, and journals and newspapers. There are some good U.S. foundations that have helped in this work. It would be better if some of the other assistance did not come from the hands of inveterate cold warriors who run the misnamed National Endowment for Democracy. These hands are soiled by years of aiding right-wing dictators and death squads. It is a standing scandal that a Democratic-controlled Congress continues to permit that agency to be run by ruthless cold warriors with a double standard where democracy is concerned. But that is by no means the worst scandal in recent U.S. performance in the areas of democracy and nonintervention.

Aid from the international financial institutions all too often is linked to such brutally onerous economic conditions that the very survival of popular and democratic regimes is put at risk. The question of how much Thatcherite social policy and austerity a newly democratic government in Eastern Europe can impose on its people and remain democratic is a difficult one. Similar ideological experiments elsewhere have not had encouraging results. Many a success story from the viewpoint of the international banking community has included sharp increases in poverty, gross income inequality, unemployment, decay of the social infrastructure, and the destruction of the trade unions. It is useful to note that when the United States tried to impose similar free-market, ideologically inspired nostrums on war-ravaged Western Europe and Great Britain as a condition for reconstruction aid after World War II, it ran into massive and successful resistance from not only the parties and unions of the working-class left but also from the Catholic parties and unions. The cold war and the need for a North Atlantic alliance convinced the United States to back down. The Western Europe of Jean Monnet and the early founders of the European Economic Community was statist and committed to a mixed economy that included a substantial state-owned sector, an extensive welfare state, and a Keynesian fiscal policy. *That* reality of a neocorporatist Western Europe, and not a Milton Friedmanite free-market utopianism, was the basis for the European economic miracle, the longest sustained period of growth in modern history.

In destroying the illusory myths of centrally planned economies or the Yugoslav version of a self-managing, social-agreement-based economy, it is essential not to fall into the opposite myth of the invisible hand, the self-regulating impartial free market. That free market never existed outside textbooks; it certainly does not exist in any major industrial democracy. If there is to be a market economy in the fragile new Eastern European democracies it should be a *social market economy*. Sweden, Austria, and even West Germany are more appropriate economic and social role models for Eastern Europe than either Great Britain or the United States. There are many reasons for this. One that I will argue is now poorly understood in the Anglo-Saxon countries, although some of the founding fathers of the United States understood it well. It is that large differences in economic status are inconsistent with genuine democracy. For that matter significant inequality in social status, access to schools and medical care, and income usually also translate into political inequality. Great economic inequality is almost always accompanied by inequality in political power. At the very least it weakens the fabric of social solidarity, without which it is hard to imagine a community that can develop the minimal notion of the common good; and without this basis it is difficult to maintain legitimate democratic authority. This is true for a host of reasons, some of which are historical.

There is a democratic tradition in Eastern Europe. Learning an Anglo-American-centered view of the world, to the extent that one learns history at all, makes one more pessimistic than one should be about the prospects for democracy in Eastern Europe and the Soviet Union. (As an aside, let me make clear that I use the term Anglo-American with an apology. Despite its popular use in the United States, the term "American" is offensive to Latin and Central Americans as well as to Canadians. It is almost as if, say, the Germans decided to call themselves Europeans and denied the applicability of that term to others. But what can one do? The constant use of the abbreviation "U.S." is stylistically clumsy.) That is because "our" history of democracy is based on a Whig theory of history, of democracy as almost an Anglo-American invention. That view not only leads to a historical hostility to great democratic revolutions, precisely as instruments of expanding democratic rights, but also explains in part the American hostility to the national liberation struggles throughout the Third World. Democracy is viewed as a set of rules of the game, as having little to do with outcomes. In addition to being narrow, this view is ethnocentric and leaves no room for the history of Hussite and Protestant rebellions in Bohemia, Hungary, and Poland, which were roughly contemporaneous with the rise of Protestant parliamentary power in England. Nor is there room in this stance for the fact that in these countries, which were long considered somehow intransigently anti-Semitic, the nobility-dominated estates of Poland, Hungary, Transylvania, and Moldavia offered religious tolerance and shelter to the Jews who fled Western European persecutions. For that matter this viewpoint reflects a poor grasp of U.S. history, since it overlooks the waves of democracy-seeking immigrants starting with the pre-revolutionary period and including distinguished Polish generals who came to the aid of American revolutionary forces.

The Polish democratic revolts in the late eighteenth and early nineteenth century are unknown to most Americans, who think of these countries as having no democratic tradition. The Austrian part of Austro-Hungary evolved far in the direction of multiethnic pluralistic parliamentarianism. For that matter little Serbia in the Balkans had a respectable parliamentary democracy for two decades before World War I. Bulgaria was an excellent example of nation building in its advance from a misgoverned Ottoman province in 1876 to a relatively constitutional monarchy. Czechoslovakia was an exemplary parliamentary democracy between the wars, until it was sold out to Hitler's Germany at Munich by France and Britain. The region was full of struggling cooperative movements, democratic peasant parties, Social Democratic parties and trade unions, and other democratic movements right up to the imposition of communist regimes after the end of World War II.

Thus this region is not without its own democratic traditions on which it can build. It is also true that it is culturally very much a part of Europe, increasingly so with the revolution in media and communications. And after all, with few exceptions, communist dictatorships were imposed from the outside with considerable U.S. and British complicity, and maintained in these countries by external Soviet force. The best ev-

idence of that is that when the reformist Gorbachev came to power in
Moscow these regimes began to collapse. With the exception of Romania they fell with surprisingly little violence—with less violence, let it be
noted, than accompanied the toppling of many Latin American dictatorships.

These postcommunist regimes will have difficulty in developing
tolerant pluralist political cultures, which require compromise and tolerance of alternative views. However, after the collapse of communism
as an ideological system what remained was all too often nationalism
and religion. Neither is necessarily tolerant. In Poland, for example, the
church and its allies are working to ban abortion. That would mean imposing Catholic doctrine, for nationalistic as well as religious reasons,
on believers and nonbelievers, on Catholics and non-Catholics. Let us
be charitable and assume that advocates of this ban propose to accom-
plish it through a democratic vote or referendum. This should come as
no surprise, since opposition to abortion is the declared official doctrine of the president of the United States and his party. How forcing
women to have unwanted children is consistent with democracy is a
mystery, in postcommunist Poland and Yugoslavia as well as in a noncommunist United States. The ban on abortions was one of the most
hated measures of the Ceauşescu dictatorship in Romania. It would be
intolerable if it were to be imposed in parts of Eastern Europe and Yugoslavia as a result of democratic reforms. This issue is a useful re-
minder that democracy is not merely simple majority rule; it must include rights and protection for those who disagree and for minorities. It
should also put into perspective the demand of the Serbian party organization in Yugoslavia that the one-person, one-vote system be imposed
in a multi-national federal state. Otherwise, smaller national groups and
republics would be doomed to the status of perpetual minorities enjoying only those rights the majority was willing to grant.

This question will keep resurfacing in Eastern Europe and Yugoslavia as they move further into democratization. What can majorities in
complex societies legitimately legislate? Can the majority by referendum, as is being proposed in Romania, ban and criminalize the Communist party? Can it outlaw abortion, as HDZ in Croatia proposes? Can
the majority limit the rights of the Muslim minority, as is proposed in
Bulgaria? Can the Serbs limit the democratic rights to self-determination of the Albanians in Kosovo by simply reintegrating that province
into Serbia and thus turning the Albanians into a minority? Can the ruling Communist party legitimately insist on cumbersome legalistic reg-
istration procedures for all new political groups and parties? For that
matter, can there be democratic elections while the party keeps a near

monopoly on the mass media and has vast properties and funds? These and similar questions will have to be answered if democracy and pluralism are to be more than abstractions. The answers are not easy or obvious.

The future of postcommunist Romania is probably one of a noncompetitive limited pluralism with elements of both corporatism and corruption, something not too different from the PRI (Institutional Revolutionary Party) in Mexico. In Bulgaria modest reforms have already been flawed by nationalistic demonstrations, organized and manipulated by local communist bureaucracies, against Turkish and other minorities. Throughout the region there is an antidemocratic alliance of traditional atavism with thinly disguised hard-line communism. This is, alas, all too familiar to Yugoslavia, which has in Serbia its own alliance of national populism and party hard-liners. Interestingly, too, popular hostility to historically dominant groups, whether Albanian or southern Slav, fuels nationalism. That hostility to the cultural and religious "other" is also tearing apart Soviet Transcaucasia. It seems that nationalistic disputes are multiplied when the factor of Christian-Muslim rivalry is added. In Transcaucasia *glasnost* has permitted the expression of age-old hatreds and grievances, and popular nationalist demands in Christian Georgia and Armenia that accounts be settled with their Muslim minorities caused two hundred thousand embittered refugees to flee to Azerbaijan. In Azerbaijan *glasnost* has led to a general opening up of the society, but this greater permissiveness as a result caused traditional national hatreds and the expression of grievances by the Armenian refugees to overflow into anti-Armenian pogroms, which then necessitated the intervention of the Soviet army. Nationalistic resistance to Soviet troops in turn leads to closer ties of the embittered Azerbaijanis with fellow Muslims in fundamentalist Iran. Clearly the beginning of democratization or *glasnost*, does not necessarily lead to the expression of democratic values.

In fairness it should be added that many of the Communist reformers have evolved in their politics to a point where they are genuine defenders of pluralistic democracy and have become democratic Socialists. But outside of the western republics of Yugoslavia these persons are the exceptions and are very rarely the *leaders* of the official reformed parties. To be sure, democratic Socialists exist inside the ruling party in the Soviet Union, where the Democratic Platform held a conference in January 1990 and brought together in-party democratic oppositional activists with a number of prominent intellectuals and opposition deputies in the Supreme Soviet. They will work for change inside the party; failing that, they propose to become the nucleus of a democratic and socialist opposition. In other countries democratic Socialists may find that it makes more sense politically to break from even the most reformed of Communist parties and move to more congenial surroundings. In East Germany, for example, the very popular mayor of Dresden has announced his shift from the reformed old Communist party (now named the Party of Democratic Socialism) to the newly organized Social Democratic party of the GDR. This move may be the beginning of a migration. But even the move to social democracy is done to maintain the left. Much of the democratic opposition is ambivalent if not hostile to *any* kind of left, even the most democratic, and violently hostile to the Communists. This hostility is one of the historical penalties to be paid for the dull drab years of communist dictatorship, and those who do not explicitly break with that past will pay a political price for some time in the future.

My reason for this historical excursion is to make two central points. First, the "West," particularly the United States, shares in the moral and political responsibility for the communist regimes in Eastern Europe. It participated in the deals that set them up, and the cold war helped these regimes to survive as the two rival superpowers developed an almost symbiotic relationship. Second, one of the mechanisms for avoiding the issue of responsibility is to claim that these countries have no natural talent or predilection for democracy. That is reserved for us. Both issues point to the original sin of U.S. foreign policy; namely, it accepted that the victorious superpowers had a right to divide Europe after the war without consulting the people involved, and it considers democracy to be reserved for developed industrialized Western nations. This is why the Bush administration is so skeptical about the prospects for democratic renewal in former communist countries, and that is why it has continued to do business with all kinds of undemocratic governments and forces—nota bene, communist antidemocratic forces and regimes when strategically useful, as the scandalous relationship of the United States to China and Pol Pot's butchers in Cambodia illustrates. I stress these matters to make my central point, which links the issue of transformations in Eastern Europe and the Soviet Union with the end of the cold war—that is, the urgent need for a new U.S. foreign policy. Such a foreign policy is essential if the United States is to maintain friendly close relations with the unified Europe that is emerging.

A new democratic foreign policy is needed. Any foreign policy we could call democratic would involve furthering democratic transformations wherever they take place with aid and moral support. This policy would work on the assumption that a world of democratic states in which military intervention is outlawed is the most secure environment for a democratic United States. This in turn would require that we give up all illusions of empire and also the notion that the United States has the natural right to interfere by armed force in small foreign countries when it pleases, on as large a scale and as ruthlessly as it chooses. To our shame it must be acknowledged that the brutal and illegal invasion of Panama was immensely popular, and raised President Bush's rating in the polls, which might lead us to question just how congruent our own present political culture is with democracy in a post-cold war world. While military nonintervention is the key to a new policy, it must include an end to the present dangerous policy of building armies throughout Latin America that are a standing menace to democracy. These armies fight only one kind of war, a savage one against their own peoples, since no credible external security threat to their counties exists, particularly now with the end of the cold war retiring right-wing fantasies of Soviet invasions. One could be cynical and contend that if an external threat exists it comes from the United States; the internal threat comes from U.S.-trained military organizations and the death squads.

This must be said, since the development of democratic states in Eastern Europe and in the Soviet Union itself depends on continued Soviet forbearance to use force against developments it finds objectionable. While they clearly had to intervene in the Armenian-Azerbaijani massacres, the Soviets have kept their hands off Eastern Europe, despite continual provocations by revanchist anticommunist crowds. This is a lesson the United States might learn.

While not doing any active harm is a good place to begin for a new foreign policy, it cannot be limited to this. There are crucial ways in which the United States can influence international financial institutions and its own banks to give the new post-cold war order, the new democracies, and decent Third World regimes a chance. This requires abolishing the immense debts that are crushing both the Eastern European countries and Third World nations. In practice much of the debt has been written off; banks should be forced to write off the rest. I argue later in this book that this is not even a question of generosity, nor is there anything wrong with generosity inspiring foreign or domestic policy. It is in the immediate self-interest of the world economy and above all the industrial North, which faces recession, to reflate world trade. Countries drowning in debt and interest payments cannot order goods and services. Many of these debts have been paid through high interest long ago, and many of these loans were pressed on Third World countries when the United States needed to do something with vast sums of petrodollars. In any case a situation in which an increasingly impoverished South is a net exporter of capital to the North is intolerable. Such a world cannot and should not be secure.

After nonintervention and eliminating the Third World and Eastern European debt, a new U.S. foreign and security policy must do something about the grotesque military budget. I discuss the issue of security at length in this book, but I want to make it clear that two outrageous things are going on in the field of defense policy today. The proposed cuts are niggardly because no genuine justification has been made for stated U.S. security needs. Defense is no mere budgetary issue; doctrine is more important. What is the doctrine behind our carrier fleets? Behind the presence of the Seventh Fleet in the Mediterranean, behind the vast U.S. forces in Western Europe? Why do we keep troops in Korea, and what is the doctrine that requires our bases in the Philippines? There may be reasons for all these, but they have certainly not been argued for in the light of recent developments. How do we justify keeping the triad of nuclear launchers on land, in submarines, and in the strategic air forces? What earthly use are the already obsolete Stealth bombers and fighter bombers? The fact that it was the Stealth that was used in the Panama operetta, although Panamanian forces had no radar, should warn us of how desperately thin the justification is for this particular boondoggle. Not only are cuts far too small, but without any real debate it is clear that the so-called peace dividend is slated mainly to pay off bond holders—that is, to reduce the artificially created U.S. deficit—rather than to turn to long-unresolved problems of the American society. We have a chance, with no credible external threat, to turn to rebuilding our infrastructure, eliminating poverty (which is fully within the realm of the possible), and building a decent health and education system. If we accomplished this we would begin catching up with the more advanced industrial democracies in Western Europe. Our educational system is probably the greatest priority, since it is the invincible ignorance of much of our electorate that permits our political system to shame American democracy. A democracy requires that there be policy debate and that alternatives be posed. This is not only true in former communist countries. We need democratic debate in the United States about defense and foreign policy. I hope this book contributes to the political debate we must have if we are to begin developing a foreign policy worthy of a democratic United States of America.

I make no pretense to impartiality or disinterested scholarship in this work. I am suspicious of works of political analysis and theory that claim such impartiality. Much of it is clearly political in its judgments and above all in its implicit and explicit preferences and prescriptions. I try to make my viewpoint as clear as I can. In a nutshell I write as a university teacher, a former union organizer, and a political activist who has spent most of his life as an engaged democratic Socialist and critical Marxist. My views are not limited in application to Western Europe or to the United States, where I teach. On the contrary, I have always felt that the most desirable path for Yugoslavia, my country of origin where I spend much of my life, is through pluralist multiparty parliamentary democracy toward a popular and democratically legitimated democratic socialism. That socialism must not only make a fundamental break with remaining elements of authoritarian Leninism, but must develop a democratic society that is both prosperous *and* practices social justice and egalitarianism.

A number of friends and colleagues were most helpful with advice and suggestions. None are responsible for the views and conclusions in this book, for which the blame is mine alone. I benefited from discussion and advice of my younger colleague John Mason, whose excellent study of French defense policy clearly influenced mine. Irving Howe, the editor of *Dissent*, has tried over the years to improve my writing and sharpen my analysis, with mixed results. My research assistants, Kim Adams and Neil McLaughlin, at the Graduate School of City University of New York have been of great help, reading and criticizing the early chapters.

New York City, January 1990

THE
END
OF THE
COLD
WAR

European Unity:
A Unique Historical Opportunity

In 1989, historic events in both Eastern and Western Europe began ac-
celerating at a breathtaking pace. Three developments, each of which by
itself would represent a major breakthrough, started unfolding ever
more rapidly. All three, interrelated as they are, represent dramatic
changes in the world political and social order established at the end of
World War II. I refer, of course, to the collapse of the ideological and political hegemony of the Communists in Eastern Europe; the end of the
cold war as we have known it between the Eastern and Western blocs led
by the Soviet Union and the United States, respectively; and the coming
economic and political integration of Western Europe, which undoubt-
edly will result in the more gradual integration of Europe as a whole. In
other words, this initially economic integration will bring about the evolution of the political and, therefore necessarily, the social and cultural
unity of Europe. The Europe that emerges will be independent of the
two superpowers, both of whose influence will decline.

To be sure, these events are all occurring within a world economy
that remains firmly capitalist, as well as increasingly global. Previous
abortive attempts to establish an autarkic set of state "socialist" economies under communist regimes are ending as their leaders implicitly
or even explicitly admit defeat by moving toward marketizing their
economies and moving them into the single world market. The marginal holdouts, like Castro in Cuba, and the squalid Albanian and North
Korean Stalinist dictatorships, only emphasize that the bulk of the communist world is moving toward marketization and other economic reforms. These reforms will not be consistent, unidirectional, or necessarily accompanied by political liberalization and democratization, as

3

the bloody debacle in Beijing's Tiananmen Square in 1989 illustrates all too clearly. There is less of a necessary link between introducing elements of the market into Communist-run economies and democracy than ideologues of the market as the sovereign remedy for all the world's problems would have. It is the case, however, that ending the monopoly on decision making in the economy by the state, which is in turn run by a single party, is a good thing in itself and *may* bring about some liberalization that in turn can lead to broader and more democratic reforms.

European unification, starting with the integration of the European Economic Community (EEC) in 1992, forms the backdrop for any consideration of the prospects and strategies of the social movements, trade unions, and labor-based and Social Democratic parties and movements anywhere in the world. They are of most urgent theoretical interest and immediate strategic relevance to such movements in the advanced industrial societies of Western Europe. History plays fair, it seems: movements do get second and even third chances, even if they do not deserve them. Western European social democracy movements, having failed to make a daring attempt to transform their societies following the Russian Revolution and World War I, did get a second chance after World War II to restructure Western Europe.

The advent of the very short-lived American century and the onset of the cold war militated against any genuinely independent role for Western Europe and therefore necessarily for Western European social democracy other than that of junior partners of the United States in the postwar Atlantic alliance of the "free world." Charles de Gaulle's bitter fulminations against a world dominated by the "Anglo-Saxon" powers and a Europe artificially and brutally divided by Yalta only confirmed those seemingly immutable realities of the postwar world order. De Gaulle turned out to be more prophetic in his definition of the problem than he was in proposing a solution. It is not de Gaulle's vision of a Europe of fatherlands that seems to be taking shape but rather a neo-Gaullist, more closely integrated "common European home" that seems to be the future of Europe. That Europe will involve considerable relinquishing of national sovereignty to an at least confederal structure for the core nations of the European Community. Quite probably there will be a number of concentric circles encompassing nations with more limited rights within this emerging Europe, but this Europe will not be confined to the western portion of the continent. It will most certainly not be limited to the Europe that is currently allied with the United States.

Today Europe itself and social democracy in Western Europe are being presented with a third chance to play a decisive role on the world scene. If they try to use that chance to develop a common European home, politics as we have known it since the end of World War II will be dramatically transformed. The year 1992 therefore represents one of those historic turning points that will effect far-reaching changes in how we think of the world. In short, just as it was "normal" to think of the world as essentially dominated by the United States and the Soviet Union (and their alliances), it will become commonplace to conceive of a Europe independent of the two superpowers. In short, the central paradigm of how we understand the world order will change.

Europe, beginning with a united economic community (the EEC), in 1992 will be economically *more* powerful than *either* the United States or the Soviet Union. This factor alone would make 1992 important. However, the fact that this occurs when the two superpowers are declining in relative strength signals a major shift in power on a global scale. In a less militarily confrontational world, both the United States and the Soviet Union will become less important, since *both* are superpowers primarily by virtue of their immense military might. For some decades this power has been paid for with relative economic and moral decline. The cost of maintaining enormous military arsenals, crippling as it was to the Soviet Union, has also weakened the United States, both economically and socially.

An exorbitant military budget was used to justify an assault on the welfare state, and this has produced an ever meaner and more divided American society. Basic research, essential to a dynamic economy and society, has steadily fallen behind. So has the funding of the basic infrastructures of a decent modern society. The educational system in the United States is a standing scandal and has contributed significantly to hard-core unemployment and the growth of an urban underclass. This process has a long history and is common to both Democratic and Republican administrations.

President Lyndon Johnson, in seeking to keep the war in Vietnam minimally acceptable to American voters, refused to pay for the American imperial adventure through higher taxes. The resulting economic burden not only devastated the social programs of the "Great Society" but also weakened both the economy and the North Atlantic alliance. The economy was weakened because of the usual political cowardice of politicians who were typically unwilling to accept any pain, such as higher taxes for policies they supported, and this in turn made inflation inevitable. At the same time, the lack of decent universal social programs made medical care and pensions a penalty paid by unionized

employers whose workers were better paid. This helped speed the transnational corporations in the process of exporting jobs to areas in which
such penalties did not exist, namely, to the newly industrialized countries (NICs) and to states that advertised a "union-free environment."
This resulted in the devastation of the midwestern industrial states and
created the "rust bowl."

The alliance was weakened in two very important ways in the 1960s
by the American preoccupation with the seemingly endless and unwin-
nable war in Vietnam. The European allies became understandably ever
more reluctant to subsidize the American adventures in Vietnam by
supporting an overvalued dollar. More important in the long run were
growing European doubts about the reliability and good sense of their
American ally, which the removal of U.S. forces from Western Europe for
the sake of the war in Vietnam raised. Obviously, if the troops could be
spared for such a sideshow (which was irrelevant to European security),
perhaps they had been unnecessary in the first place. Doubts about the
need to maintain a powerful conventional military presence in Europe
in turn led to dangerous and increasingly unpopular ideas about the potential feasibility of nuclear weapons in Europe, specifically, intermedi-
ate-range nuclear weapons.

The proposition that Europe, particularly crowded Central Europe,
was a potential, even probable, *nuclear* battlefield began to sink in as
the consequences of the U.S. policymakers' strategic shift away from the
nuclear deterrence of mutual assured destruction (MAD) to the new
nuclear utilization theory and strategy (NUTS) became clearer. This
growing awareness guaranteed massive opposition throughout the
1970s and early 1980s to the deployment of U.S. nuclear missiles in Europe, further eroding the moral basis of the alliance, on the one hand,
and raising the specter of truly massive military spending cuts (the so-
called zero option) on the other. In other words, it created a situation in
which the Gorbachev peace initiative was a Soviet opportunity waiting
to happen.

With the military might of the superpowers becoming less significant, their roles are declining and their weaknesses becoming more salient. Their weaknesses are very similar. They both carry a dispropor-
tionate share of the military burden in their respective alliances. They
are also increasingly less attractive as models and leaders of alliances.
While the Soviet Union is incomparably worse off economically, the
United States is becoming less and less attractive socially and politically. The hypocrisy of U.S. political leaders, both Democratic and Republican, in backing murderous right-wing regimes in Latin America
and other Third World nations while preaching the supreme virtues of

democracy is matched only by the seaminess of the decade-long assault on already modest domestic social welfare programs.

During the long Reagan years over $57 billion was cut from social programs that were already miserly compared to those of the advanced Western European industrial states. This has created among other things a housing crisis on a scale unknown in the First World. One hundred thousand homeless men, women, and children in New York City alone are part of the price to be paid for the ideologically inspired assault on a barely existing welfare state and on a modest federal housing program, both of which have been devastated by funding cuts. It is hard to imagine a nation claiming to be the leader of the free world that has a horrendous crime rate, massive and increasingly visible homelessness, and a rapidly growing gap between the rich and poor. It does not help that it is also the country in which a decade-long assault on workers' rights and trade unions has been carried out.

This offensive against workers' rights and unions would be loudly denounced by U.S. spokespersons were it to take place under any communist regime. It boggles the imagination to consider what the reaction of the U.S. political leaders and press would be if a communist regime murdered priests and nuns the way our squalid dependency in El Salvador does. Worse, it is conceivable that the United States would be silent if and only if that communist regime served the needs of U.S. foreign policy (as we saw in the scandalous military and diplomatic support for the genocidal Khmer Rouge in Cambodia). All this adds to a United States that is less and less able to lead any alliance—least of all an alliance of parliamentary democracies in a Western Europe dominated by the broad democratic left, the Social Democrats, and the Greens.

European Unification:
The Changing Social and Political Terrain

The increased economic and political integration of the European Community in 1992, combined with the ever-greater penetration of national economies by the world market, clearly dictates less national and parochial strategies to Western European labor movements and parties. A shift in strategies is essential in order to be able to deal with the multinationals, the mobility of labor, and the constant danger of the flight of capital that threaten existing welfare states and social programs. This necessarily means that it will become increasingly less relevant to think in terms of social policies, trade union goals, and the range of social and economic policy options in terms of single nation-states. The European Community itself will be the narrower arena in which those issues, or at least the major parameters of those issues, will be debated for the remainder of this century. This will initially encompass Western Europe, and possibly all of Europe by the end of the century.

This growing unification of Europe in no way precludes numerous bitter local and national struggles over issues of social policy and economic equity. In all probability most of the struggles will occur within these more familiar and comfortable frameworks. All that is being asserted here is that the ultimate arena in which these issues will be determined in most cases will be the larger European Community. The EEC in turn will be constrained by considerations of the world economy and market. What this specifically means is that unions and social movements, it is to be hoped in alliance and coordination, must develop stronger transnational ties and institutions. Clearly this is essential to maintain certain "European" social and economic standards and to develop codes of rights for workers and unions that would be in force across the Continent. The Community's *present* structure already provides for courts to defend human rights, and these have been used to some effect to protect political prisoners and the social and economic rights of women. Ecological concerns constitute another area in which national boundaries and legislation have little meaning, since many of the issues go beyond the Community and even beyond Europe itself. In any case, it is self-evident that ecologists must organize on a supranational basis. The imminent death of the Mediterranean demands international, not simply European, action. As the bitter experience of the Chernobyl disaster has demonstrated, antinuclear activists are obliged to think beyond the nation-state as the arena for relevant activity. For that matter Chernobyl has shown just how devilishly interlinked issues like ecology, industrial policy, and freedom of the press and information are, and radioactively contaminated trout in northern Sweden illustrate that these issues cannot be treated as the internal problems of a single nation.

The labor-based Socialist parties, as well as the Italian Communists now allied with them, are already the single largest organized political group within the European Parliament. I use the terms Social Democratic and Socialist more or less interchangeably when referring to parties and movements affiliated with the Socialist International. Since the dissolution of the Communist International and its heir, the Communist Information Bureau (the Cominform), the Socialist International represents the only more or less unified world socialist workers' movement. Despite all protestations to the contrary, the small but expanding ecologist group, the Greens, will find itself pulled into an alliance with this bloc. This is a growing trend that was confirmed in the spring 1989 elections for the European Parliament. Internationalism and transnational organizational ties and cooperation are more ideologically congenial to the left than to the right (whose "internationalism" is more often expressed as Atlanticism).

In any case, no bloc of parties today operates in an organized manner throughout Western Europe except the Socialist parties and the institutions allied with them (e.g., International Secretariats of the International Confederations of Free Trade Unions, the ICFTU). To be sure, both seek to operate in a global context and not merely a European or "Eurocentric" one. It is the case, however, that the more effective cooperative working arrangements for both the parties and trade unions associated with European social democracy, broadly defined, are to be found in Western Europe. The more global non-European role is still more an expression of intent than a reality, although considerable and increasing aid is sent to unions and parties in the Third World, mostly in Latin American countries. Liberal and conservative parties are far more fragmented and nationally specific whereas the social Catholic parties, and the unions allied with them, are all but nonexistent in Northern Europe. The Socialist parties have a number of international coordinating bodies, for example, the Socialist International, the European Socialist Parliamentary Group, the International Federation of Socialist Women, and the International Union of Socialist Youth, through which a number of the present leaders of the parties first met. Paralleling these are the International Secretariats of the members of the ICFTU, mostly Socialist dominated, which are assuming more importance. Although these international institutions of the labor and socialist movement are often weak and largely symbolic, symbols are important and they form a stable international network linking the social democratic institutions in a way that has no parallel for the bourgeois parties. The closest equivalent would be the Catholic parties and unions. .

Even granting that a great deal of, if not most (as of now and for the immediate future), policy-making and policy-proposal generation originate within the labyrinths of the vast Eurocracy (European Common Market commissions and their bureaucracy), this does not weaken the dominant role of the pro-welfare state broad left and left-center in the EEC. This is because that bureaucracy tends to be "statist"—that is, sympathetic to an interventionist role of the state in the formation and financing of social policy. Such a view willy-nilly places the European bureaucracy in conflict with Thatcherite and other neo-Darwinian market enthusiasts and on the side of those who argue for a social Europe and for a maximalist view of what unification of the market in 1992 should include. That is, whether openly or more discreetly, Eurocrats advocate maximizing the prerogatives of the bodies of the European Community in respect to the individual member states.

Relegitimating the Democratic State and Politics

Social movements as well as the broad left must restore legitimacy to the idea that an active interventionist democratic state is essential to assure the minima of decent social and civic services a modern society needs. Grass-roots organizations and direct democracy in neighborhoods and workplaces may well be both desirable and possible. Within society as a whole—and society is clearly no longer, if it ever was, an extension of culturally and ethnically homogeneous communities in any of the modern industrial states—democracy is possible only within the framework of a democratic state, one that provides decent, universal, and not means-tested civic and social services that are democratically responsive. It is important to remember that although the left, particularly the far left, has had an authentic and vigorous antistatist and anti-institutional tradition of its own, the most widespread and politically significant discourse of antistatism during the past decade has been the language of the market-oriented right. It is worth adding that the antistatist *ideology* of the right has precious little to do with "the really existing," to borrow a phrase from communist vocabulary, right—that is, the right in power. That genuine right, rather than the one found in small intellectual journals and foundations, has used the state consistently on behalf of the rich, the greedy, and the powerful in transferring as much income and power to them as it could get away with just short of indictable actions. In their enthusiasm to use and abuse the state the right often crossed those loose boundaries of what was and was not legal. A number of its uses of the state to redistribute goods were quite shameless; witness some of the schemes to privatize natural resources and the fiddles with the tax structure to make it ever more regressive. That is only one more reason why progressives should be very skeptical about contemporary antistatist rhetoric. Possessive individualism may well be the closest thing there is to an all-American ideology. It has proved to be a social, economic, and political disaster for the vast majority.

Hostility to the state as such, without specifying what kind of state, means to abandon it to the permanent bureaucracies and small cliques

of professional politicians. It also entails legitimating right-wing assaults against the services provided by the state by ideologically permit-
ting the cloaking of these attacks as antistatist individualism and freedom. Although right-wing libertarianism does exist it has always been
an ideological fig leaf for the genuine politics of the right in advanced
capitalist states. The *real* politics of conservatives involve the systematic
use of the state, particularly its repressive capacities, to pursue the
agendas of private greed and to uphold the rules of the game, which
remain tilted in favor of the wealthy and powerful. The ultimate, of
course, is the use of the state to maintain a fundamentally unjust economic order that favors the rich *internationally.* That is one, perhaps the
only, reasonable explanation for the American love affair with the aircraft carrier as a mechanism for projecting power. Whatever these levi-
athans might have been used for originally, they were obviously useless
against a first-rate military power like the Soviet Union. On the other
hand, they did just fine in helping to win the only actual military conflict the Reagan administration fought after the huge arms buildup. I am
referring, of course, to the U.S. military "triumph" against Grenada. It
was supposed to be a lesson to small, obstreperous nations. Happily the
lesson did not take.

In the United States, antistatism of the right was singularly absent
during the multibillion dollar rescue of the savings and loan banks,
whereas libertarian antistatism was singularly absent when the
Chrysler Corporation needed government loans and help, or when the
power of the presidency was repeatedly invoked in labor disputes. Sim-
ilarly the Conservatives in Great Britain have repeatedly used the state
against unions and even more blatantly to loot nationalized industries.

However, to contest power in a large organization such as an entire
nation-state, citizens can no longer participate directly as they did in
the Greek *polis*, in intentional utopian communities like Israeli *kibbut-
zim*, or in small New England towns. For that matter they cannot do so
even in smaller units like large cities. Instead, they need to form and
democratically control political organizations, parties, and movements,
since it is only through the mediation of these that policy choices are
made coherent for citizens as a group. The whole idea of responsible
political party organization has been under continual attack from the
very foundation of parliamentary democracy. Most of those attacks are
informed by various brands of elitist thought that recoil at the very idea
of the messy political hurly-burly that party contestation at its best provides. Upper-class reformers have repeatedly assaulted real-life democracy from Plato on through the reform movements at the beginning of

this century in the United States to frankly corporatist organizations like Opus Dei.

Unfortunately the student New Left of the 1960s also joined the attack on political parties as such, fighting a limited good (i.e., liberalism and social programs) in the name of perfection (i.e., revolution). That after all was the meaning of the slogan in those magic days of May 1968 in Paris, "Be realistic, demand the impossible!" Today the most difficult task is to restore a coherent vision of a democratic and radical politics of the *possible*, a politics of social equity combined with ecological responsibility that is not limited to the rich countries of the First World. This will be a major field for intellectual and political contestation in the immediate future.

The Immediate Future: Where Is All This Going?

The next proposed expansion of the European Economic Community will include the European Fair Trade Association (EFTA), with Switzerland, Sweden, Norway, and Austria as members and with Finland and Yugoslavia as associates. This will strengthen the "natural" majority of the leftist labor-based parties within a unified Europe given the strength of those parties in most EFTA member countries. Sharply increased prospects for either a reunification of the Germanys, or at the very least a closer relationship of the German Democratic Republic to the Common Market, will further strengthen this "left" or social tilt of the European Community.

That is why ideological conservatives like Thatcher are quite justifiably increasingly both nervous about 1992 itself and scarcely European (i.e., minimalist) when it comes to the economic and social policy prerogatives of the EEC, and opposed to any plans to expand it by adding new members. Reservations about the pace of European unification are today visibly splitting Conservative party leaders in Britain. This is also why even the traditionally insular British Trades Union Congress is finally beginning to grasp the socially progressive and organizationally useful consequences of European unification, particularly for weak labor movements. That same point has been very well understood by the Mediterranean Socialist parties like those of Greece and Spain who look to the EEC to provide model social policies including pensions, minimal wages, and union rights.

Scholars and policymakers dealing with social policies and labor-based parties and movements must understand that the coming European economic unification, and the necessarily consequent increasing separation of the European Community from its traditional Atlantic alliance, will radically change the game of social politics in Europe. It will also alter a great many other heretofore solid realities of world politics and the economic balance of power. That is why that unification is historically significant. It would have been so in any case, but following as it does in the wake of the democratic earthquake in Eastern Europe and a shutting down of the cold war means that 1992 will bring an entire era to a close—the era of a world dominated by the superpowers and by the cold war.

European unification and the end of the cold war come at a time when the desperate straits of a debt-ridden Third World make necessary politically attractive and economically feasible pan-national reflationary strategies involving massive credits and aid to both Eastern Europe and the Soviet Union and the South. This aid must involve the wholesale writing-off of the crippling indebtedness of the poorer countries. International debt is an instrument through which poor countries, where the vast majority of the world's population live, have become net *exporters* of capital to the industrial and wealthy North. That is an impossible situation that cannot continue if there is to be any change for the better in the Third World. That is why progressive industrialists and bankers in the North, and there are such, join with the Socialist International and the Catholic church in calling for a new economic order, the essence of which involves wiping out these debts. Such proposals are politically attractive in Western Europe, since they represent the mix of altruism and benefit to the national economies of the advanced industrial countries in the European Community. This mix creates a sufficiently broad political base of support to make such proposals politically feasible.

The End of a Conflict:
The Catholic Church and Social Justice

Historic changes in the policies and views of the Catholic church over the past several decades have created further support for progressive economic policies toward the Third World. These changes go much further than the better publicized development of a theology of liberation, which has won support among Christian radicals. The official policies of the church itself have shifted toward a greater emphasis on social justice and equity. This raises the possibilities of an implicit or even explicit alliance between Socialists and Catholicism in three major areas: a joint concern with North/South issues in the context of accepting that the North has a major responsibility to help the South; a joint agreement on a defense of the right of workers to form and control their own unions and movements; and third, a joint concern with uniting social justice and democracy.

The two great historic movements today also agree in defending both an advanced welfare state and the right of people to decent jobs. This places both groups in conflict with the neoliberal fetishization of the market as the be-all and end-all of social and economic policy. The church no more shares the cult of the market as the supreme regulator of what is socially desirable than do the Socialists, despite the prolonged post-World War II alliance between Washington and the Vatican. It certainly does not accept that a decent society can be founded on a worldview as shallow and self-centered as the possessive individualism that seems dominant in the United States, and which seems to be one of the very few American products that is successfully exported throughout the world. Add to these broad bases of agreement a common hostility to the nuclear arms race, and to a world dominated by the superpowers, and one may well have what amounts to a historic shift in political alliances in the making.

Policymakers and political publics in the advanced industrial countries increasingly question the possibility of continuing the broad post-World War II class compromises and welfare state settlements as well as the capacity of Keynesian economic policies to manage advanced capitalist economies. Broad and growing skepticism exists about the very possibility of maintaining an advanced welfare state economically. Doubts about the viability of a welfare state have been reinforced by the wholesale attack on welfare programs and norms based on ideological conviction by the neoconservatives who have dominated British and U.S. politics in the past decade. These attacks turned out to be a form of self-fulfilling prophecy; as the ideologically inspired budgetary cuts crippled and warped the social programs of the welfare state, the remaining programs became more niggardly and inadequate. As a result they are less broadly popular and more ghettoized to poor and dependent populations.

Some observers have called this assault on the welfare state over the past decade and a half the crisis of contemporary socialism and socialist movements. It would be more accurate to talk of a crisis of socially liberal capitalism or, even more precisely, a crisis of the neocorporatism that seemed to be the all but invincible wave of the future during the 1960s and 1970s. Social democracy on the other hand, at least in the advanced industrial democracies of Western Europe, seems to be thriving. It will thus probably play a key role in the shaping of a new Europe after 1992.

Chapter 1

European Security, Unity, and the End of the Cold War

The current prognosis for a continuation of the U.S. domination of Western Europe, and for that country's ability to continue to shape the parameters of European social and economic policies, is considerably poorer than the prospects for a Europe, at least a Western Europe, dominated by labor-oriented and Socialist parties. The entire post-World War II Atlanticist cold war consensus is today undergoing a profound and probably terminal crisis and is in massive disrepair, in part because recent U.S. administrations have labored mightily (and, for all purposes, successfully) to weaken it fatally. This weakening was accomplished by acts of both omission and commission; it was also truly bipartisan.

The most consistent primary aim of Soviet foreign policy since World War II was to get the United States out of Europe. Failing that, the intermediary aim was at least to undermine its role there. That aim is well on the way to being achieved essentially through the past actions of the United States, and American policymakers are reaping the results of unease and resentment that had been building up for over two decades. In that sense Gorbachev has achieved through a conciliatory policy what decades of Soviet threats, bullying, and arms buildup could not. I argue here that a Europe independent of the United States is a very good thing for the world. Given the relations of strength and the *strategic* rather than *tactical shift in Soviet policy*, Europe will also, as a matter of course, be independent of the Soviet Union.

That Western Europeans should indefinitely and unquestioningly support cruel and cavalier American adventures throughout Latin America and increasingly dubious policies in Asia and Africa seemed self-evident to U.S. policymakers of both parties. It became more and more obvious, however, that the United States' preoccupation with low-intensity warfare in the Third World had precious little to do with the security of the Western alliance or even that of the United States itself. That preoccupation was dictated by the narrow and parochial require-ments of *internal* U.S. politics, that is, the need of neoconservatives in both parties actively to combat communism. Since direct military con-flict with the major communist power was far too dangerous (and in any case unlikely), hapless Third World surrogates would have to do. This brought about untold suffering in Angola, Namibia, Cambodia, and, above all, Central America. The more convoluted the relationship of these dirty little semiclandestine wars to any genuine security interests became, the more the support of U.S. allies waned. For some years West-ern European Social Democrats have been on a collision course with U.S. policy in the Third World. Most U.S. policymakers have blithely as-sumed that this is of no consequence. Indeed, this would *not* matter were it not for the uncomfortable additional fact that the Social Demo-crats involved are not tiny irrelevant sectaries. Instead, they represent either the government or the opposition in every major Western Euro-pean country. That makes their attitude toward U.S. policies a diplo-matic problem for the United States. The latter, however, like the Soviet Union in relation to its bloc, appears to consider diplomacy to be a game involving its own unilateral initiatives that it will communicate to it allies when it chooses to do so. This relationship is not long for this world. Europe is an economic giant in short pants, and it is rapidly out-growing American tutelage. It will soon be independent of both Wash-ington and Moscow.

That old relationship within the alliance was a reflection of a gen-uine reality in the never-to-be-repeated era when an immensely power-ful and wealthy United States, undamaged by the world war, faced a war-torn Europe and Japan that were unable to resist Soviet power. It may be hard to remember today, at the close of the American century, but the United States was not only economically supreme in the post-World War II world, it was unmatched in the type of military might necessary for global superpower status. While the Soviet Union did have more tanks and heavy artillery, the United States had a monopoly on nuclear weap-ons, and more to the point it also possessed the only previously tested way to deliver an atomic bomb to a target. In other words, it had the only strategic air force in the world as well as the only navy that could effectively project military power globally.

That era is long past, but consciousness is not alway quick to catch up to reality. There are still Americans who think they enjoy the highest standard of living in the world, for example. Nevertheless an end to its imperial role, which is disturbing to American pundits and leaders, may be very advantageous for the United States and the world. It may, although little is certain in politics, lead to a fundamental reexamination and debate about U.S. foreign and defense policies. It may raise the question of what kind of international policy is appropriate for the most powerful democracy in the world. And if, as I devoutly hope, this debate and reexamination lead to the development of a democratic foreign policy that will not make decent Americans ashamed, the United States will have gained something immensely important, namely, the regard of democratic-minded people and movements throughout the world.

Faith in the efficacy or the exportability of the Soviet and state "socialist" models of political and economic development has vanished even, or perhaps especially, within the Soviet leadership. The collapse of dictatorial communist regimes throughout most of Eastern Europe under a combination of reformist pressures from above and mass pressures from below has left an ideological vacuum. The remaining liberal communist elites are now searching for some vestige of a program that combines a vision of a better social order with the possibility of democratizing and reforming their societies so as to gain access to aid and technology from the West. Not so incidentally it is going to be considerably more difficult for regimes that stall on democratic and economic reforms to get aid. This factor has not escaped the attention of political leaders in Eastern Europe and the Soviet Union, and is one more item pressing in favor of reforms. The Soviets and their Eastern European allies increasingly look to the advanced welfare states of Scandinavia and Western Europe as the models of socially and politically *acceptable* types of market economies, that is, market economies with a mix of forms of property ownership and an advanced welfare state and strong trade unions. After all, it is hardly an open question as to which is more successful and humane as a market economy, Sweden or Thatcher's Britain.

The attempt of Hungarian Communist reformers to develop a new social democratic party, the Hungarian Socialist party, is representative. That party combines the idea of a welfare state with a market economy with mixed forms of ownership, both private and public. The raw or primitive capitalism of the socially unregulated market, as Jacques Delors, the architect of the programs for a social Europe in 1992, calls it, is unlikely to be introduced in Eastern European states.

This is the case despite the fact that many reform-minded economists and journalists in Eastern Europe often do talk in terms of a "Thatcherite" free market as being what is needed to reform their societies effectively. There are two reasons for this wholly perverse point of view. On the one hand those who advocate it simply do not grasp the social and political consequences of Thatcherite (or for that matter Reaganite) economics. That is, they imagine that what they call Thatcherism or Reaganism means some kind of almost laboratory-pure market economy and not the naked defense of greed and use of state power on behalf of the rich and powerful that is really taking place.

Second, those who promote this type of free market cannot really imagine a society or economy so barbaric as to be without those welfare state programs that are common and widely taken for granted in most of Europe, East and West. What the defenders of the "hard" market option in Eastern Europe imagine is happening in the United States and Britain is merely a verbal assault on the excesses of the welfare state accompanied by benevolent attempts to prune their surplus bureaucratic baggage.

This is in large part because Eastern European intellectuals and general populaces do not believe their own press even when it prints the truth about the realities of the capitalist world. Thus, for example, I have never been able to convince Polish, Hungarian, and Yugoslavian "free marketers" that there is widespread homelessness in the United States and that some thirty thousand persons sleep on the streets of New York, the richest city in the richest country in the world. They think this is sheer communist propaganda, whereas they *know* about the housing crisis in their own societies. On the other hand, it is hard to convince Eastern Europeans that there are those for whom the market means not only freedom from continuous interference by the state and party in every detail of the economy but also the barbaric vision of the real-life American and British conservatives in power that pensions and health benefits should be denied to those who have failed in the marketplace. They would be shocked to discover this truth about politicians like Thatcher and Reagan, whom they know only as staunch anti-Communists. Their assumption, the assumption of the naive throughout the ages, is that their enemy's enemy is necessarily their friend. This is further proof of the danger of basing policies on the devil you know. There can well be other dangers.

The social and political consequences of an assault on the crude and almost universal welfare state that exists in the Eastern European regimes would be incalculable. Democratization itself would be in real danger if it were seen as *necessarily* accompanied by massive unemployment and cutbacks in already inadequate health services and pensions. But then economic theorists almost never consider the political and social effects of the application of their theories on living societies.

Western European states with their strong unions and social movements and relatively advanced welfare systems appear to have more favorable prospects than *either* the class-confrontational neoconservative "Anglo-Saxons" or the economically ruined state socialist polities of Eastern Europe and the Soviet Union. It is not *capitalism* that has won the cold war, as some Western pundits claim. Rather it is authoritarian state socialism that has *lost* the cold war. But it has lost it to Western European *welfare state* capitalism, run as often as not, by Social Democratic and Labor parties—in short, to a form of neocorporatism that is much influenced by and tilted in favor of organized labor and its allies through broad social programs and industrial relations legislation modifying the raw forces of the market. This was accomplished through the political strength of the Social Democratic parties and the organizational strength of the unions and social movements.

Military Cutbacks and European Security

Responding to massive economic and ideological crises Soviet leadership under Mikhail Gorbachev has shown itself to be extraordinarily open at this time to far-reaching political and economic reforms as well as to radical cutbacks in military expenditures and arsenals. The first and most visible evidence of the seriousness with which the Soviets approach these reforms is just emerging. It should be obvious that the changes that are sweeping Eastern Europe would be impossible without Soviet approval or at least acceptance. True, the Soviet need to reduce spending is urgent. It is not merely that massive costs are involved in maintaining huge and unnecessary military establishments. The problem is that the relative costs of maintaining the Soviet Union as a superpower matching the United States are far greater than the equivalent cost to the United States. To begin with, the Soviet economy is less than half the size of that of the United States. Even more important is that since becoming a superpower at the close of World War II, the Soviet Union has had to allocate the lion's share of its best scientists and engineers as well as material resources to the military to remain competitive with the United States and Western Europe. Therefore any major move to reform the Soviet economy necessarily requires shifting massive resources—material and human—from the military to the civilian sectors.

This has been well understood for decades by Western analysts of Soviet society. It has not, however, prevented three American presidents in a row from promoting an arms race in the name of security. It is not at all difficult, therefore, to imagine a Soviet leadership concerned with strengthening and modernizing its economy proposing drastic military cutbacks. This also, incidentally, underscores the position of those in the Soviet military who advocate a more modern military establishment after a more realistic assessment of Soviet security needs has been made. The military bureaucracy in the Soviet Union (*and* of course in the United States) will continue to fight for its relative share of funding and hardware. To modernize one must therefore cut back. For example, without getting rid of it aircraft carriers the United States can never have a technologically and strategically contemporary navy. Without cutting back on the artifacts of a war fought like World War II (i.e., tanks and heavy artillery), the Soviets cannot modernize their forces without crippling their economy. Military thinkers in the Soviet Union are well aware that their country cannot remain a first-class power *even militarily* without modernizing its economy. For this reason they support Gorbachev and the plan to bring about deep cuts in armaments, and thus the present policy is likely to be a long-range one that would even survive the fall of Gorbachev.

However, the most powerful argument that supports Soviet policymakers who agree with Gorbachev's military cutbacks, as well as Western Europeans who keep pressing for matching cuts on the part of NATO, is a simple political reality that has finally begun to sink in after long decades of the cold war. It is quite simple: a war of any kind in Europe between the two alliances is extremely unlikely. The Continent is the least likely place on earth for a military conflict between the superpowers, either directly or through surrogates. This strengthens Western advocates of disarmament and the tendency for Western Europe toward greater autonomy within the traditional North Atlantic alliance.

The notion that the Soviet Union is increasingly less dangerous to Western security interests is even accepted by U.S. policymakers, including Dick Cheney, the current secretary of defense. Cheney drew a logical conclusion from this new view of an old reality and in November of 1989 exposed the American military, used to ever growing "defense" budgets, to what amounted to systemic shock when he ordered it to come up with budget reductions amounting to $180 billion by 1994. That budget is already so monstrously bloated that this is still a very modest cutback. Proposals are on the table at the Office of Management and Budget calling for far more substantial cuts.

It is even possible that the Democrats in Congress *might*, for once begin to act as an opposition party and make their own proposals. Everything is possible in politics, or almost everything. After all, if the Communists can permit elections in Eastern Europe, why would something like the emergence of a genuine opposition party in the United States be a fantasy? In any case, the time is obviously ripe for a hostile examination of the herd of sacred cows that have grazed and grown fat on the military budget for so long. Military stocks have fallen in value. Under those circumstances major cuts in military appropriations and expenditures are all but guaranteed. The optimal way for this to take place would be to force a discussion, not about the numbers in the budget, but about the strategic assumptions behind any reasonable military policy, if there is such a thing. In other words, what is needed is to force the U.S. military to articulate a rationale for what American *aims* should be, a rationale from which military *needs* are deduced and from which in turn hardware and personnel needs can be determined; from this process one could then derive some budgetary estimates. In short, the argument should not be about what various weapon systems *cost*, but rather, what they are *for*. The question, in other words, is what conceivable legitimate policy aim is served, and in particular, what legitimate policy aim of a *democratic* state is served?

In this way truly spectacular cuts could be placed on the American agenda as one raises fundamental questions. One can ask, what is the purpose of maintaining any conventional American forces in Europe at all, not how can costs be pared? Another logical question is, why does the United States, or the "West" for that matter, need a dozen aircraft carrier *groups*? What conceivable scenario or contingency are they for? Then one could start asking some really basic questions about *security*. Why *not* negotiate strategic and other nuclear weapons away, or at least down to the minimal deterrent of a few hundred missiles per superpower (which most experts think would assure a balance)? Why not trade off entire systems of weapons, strategic bombers, intermediate nuclear weapons (whatever that grotesque notion ever meant), and give up all capabilities for poison gas and germ warfare? If no major war is anticipated between the superpowers and their alliances, then *security* forces for the needs of an essentially noninterventionist United States or Soviet Union can become quite modest indeed. Sufficiency to assure the safety of the nation and allies and to discourage military adventures of small or medium-size powers would call for defense forces and budgets many times smaller than the present ones.

This also means that pressure by the United States on the West Germans and other European allies to increase their military budgets is politically as dead as a doornail. There is no political support for this proposition, which was in trouble even before the Gorbachev peace initiative went into high gear. It will be more and more difficult to get Western

Europeans to maintain large military budgets when no danger is evident.

The United States will be increasingly isolated internationally if it does not begin to develop some equivalent of a diplomatic "peace initiative" of its own. President Bush's statement that Gorbachev would be taken seriously when the Berlin Wall was removed and when free elections were permitted in Eastern Europe has returned to haunt him. Where are the moves the United States has taken? The rest of the world does not share the view so taken for granted by American political leaders that the United States symbolizes peaceful rectitude, nonintervention, and support for democracy. There have been no unilateral initiatives on the part of the United States that match the Soviet withdrawal from Afghanistan. The United States has not even stopped sending military aid to the rebel factions it supports there. Why doesn't the United States pull down its "wall" against Cuba and Nicaragua, thereby ending the undeclared but very real economic war against those countries? Couldn't the Bush administration genuinely cut off military, financial, and political support to the cut-throats, killers, death squads, and the governments backing them, all over Central and Latin America?

There is little or no chance, however, of the Bush administration doing anything of the sort. The brutal torture and murder of the Jesuits in El Salvador by U.S.-trained and -financed killers in army uniforms, and the January 1990 ambushing of nuns in Nicaragua by U.S.-funded contras, continue to be treated with more or less benign tolerance. When it comes to these killings, the official U.S. spokespersons show a presumption of innocence until absolute proof of guilt is produced, which would strain the credulity of even the most enthusiastic members of the American Civil Liberties Union. Instead of reacting to these outrageous violations of human rights by armed thugs, actions for which the United States bears a clear moral and political responsibility, American officials expose terrified Salvadorans who witnessed the murder of the Jesuits to brutally threatening interrogation on U.S. soil by the Salvadoran political police.

Nothing illustrates the increasingly shabby international role of the United States as clearly as the illegal armed intervention in Panama at the end of 1989. This intervention also illustrates the extent to which U.S. foreign policy is subordinated to parochial national politics.[1] While *all* Latin American countries, and the entire non-aligned bloc and the large majority of the UN General Assembly, denounced the invasion, the media focus in the United States was on the support for the invasion *in the United States* and the increase in President Bush's domestic popularity ratings.

To get rid of one squalid military dictator, himself clearly a product of U.S. and CIA policies in Panama and formerly on the payroll of the CIA (which sponsored his rise in Panamanian politics and the military), the United States deployed over 28,000 troops on foreign soil and engaged in the wholesale destruction of lives and property. Hundreds of lives paid for President Bush's preoccupation with the challenge to U.S. prestige on the part of a thug who would not stay bought. The entire Panama operation has an odious smell of hypocrisy in the light of U.S. kowtowing to the Chinese hard-liners before the blood in Beijing's Tiananmen Square dried, not to mention the continued, albeit indirect, support for Pol Pot's butchers in Cambodia. The number of dictators and corrupt drug profiteers the United States has supported is not small, without even raising the genuinely ugly issue of CIA involvement in drug trafficking in the Far East, in the Golden Triangle.

Even more preposterous is the supposed legal justification for the invasion, namely, that General Noriega was under indictment in the United States. That is unbelievable effrontery. On what earthly basis does American leadership assume the right to indict foreign nationals, on foreign soil, and insist on *its* right to remove them by military force in order to try them in the United States? Can one just imagine what would happen if, let us say, the Soviet Union claimed such a right in Eastern Europe? The claim would be rightly rejected with indignation by world public opinion. Protection of American lives, the second justification for the invasion, is hardly a convincing argument. Many more lives were lost through the intervention than would have been otherwise, even if the United States does not, as it obviously does not, count mere Panamanian civilian and military lives as part of the cost. In any case, U.S. hostages continue to face death and imprisonment throughout the Middle East, without any visible efforts to end their misery by this or previous administrations.

Morally outrageous as the virtual kidnapping of Noriega and the invasion of Panama was, it is something even worse: it was a blunder, it was genuinely stupid. Hostility to the United States throughout Latin America will justifiably rise. The invasion will fail to achieve its strategic aim, which, let us remember, was to win the "war" against drugs. The United States is rebuilding the same brutal, corrupt, drug-dealing Panamanian defense force that was Noriega's base of power. It is thus recreating the same kind of Frankenstein's monster Noriega had turned out to be. The only policy consistent with giving democracy and civilian government any kind of fighting chance in Panama has been proposed by Senator Dodd. It is as simple as it is obvious. Panama should be encouraged to be like Costa Rica, that is, to have no army at all. There is no credible military threat to either Panama or the canal, other than the United States, of course. However, the American-armed, -trained, and -supported military throughout Latin America remains a threat to democracy.

Although American leaders continue to dither in the face of dramatic events in Eastern Europe and the Soviet peace initiatives, they cannot filter out all political considerations and the increasing restiveness of their allies. The United States will be dragged toward ever larger military cutbacks, but its obvious reluctance will diminish any political credit it gets for these cuts. They will be seen as being grudgingly wrung from an averse leadership by the inexorable development of events. Nevertheless the cuts in military spending by the United States and in Western European countries, as well as by the Soviet Union, will be real. In turn, the reductions will lead to a gradual end of the cold war and open exciting possibilities for continued democratic change in Eastern Europe and the Soviet Union. Extensive long-range credits on favorable terms will probably be offered to Soviet leaders to aid the modernization of their economy and society. Such a policy would also help Western European economies much like the Marshall Plan in the 1940s helped the U.S. economy. One clear effect of a modern-day "Marshall Plan" would be to reflate the economies sufficiently to increase employment and growth; this, combined with the savings resulting from military cutbacks that are inevitable in an era of increasing detente, would generate additional resources for politically popular social expenditures and welfare measures, without requiring politically unpopular tax increases.

The Domestic Impact of Military Cutbacks

Under such circumstances attacks on the welfare state clearly become a matter of harsh antiwelfare ideology rather than the supposed unfortunate side effect of economic necessity imposed by the voracious appetite of a defense budget. This is why Thatcherism is now on the defensive in Britain and why the electoral chances of the Labour party are sharply improving. More generally this is also why demands for a "social Europe" meet with wide support and little organized hard-core hostility. In periods of general prosperity, particularly those underpinned by the state-supported priming of the economy through large loans, neocorporatist strategies of class compromise are more likely than confrontational assaults on unions and social standards.

This is true, of course, of "normal" modern capitalists but not necessarily of right-wing ideologues who have dominated politics, and above all the political debate, in Great Britain and the United States. That era is likely to end with the close of the cold war. Class-confrontational politics of the Anglo-Saxon type never really took hold in Western Europe and are clearly out of place in an essentially bureaucratic and neocorporatist EEC.

Western Europe is crucial for both the fate and future of advanced welfare states and democratic Socialist parties. But for Western Europe to be able to assume such a role it must first free itself from the tutelage and domination of the United States. For U.S. military protection to be perceived as no longer necessary, it is essential that Western Europeans feel sufficiently secure from the military threat and potential political bullying of the Soviet Union. The ideal time for this is a period of major military cutbacks and disarmament of the superpowers in Europe. These reductions are accompanied by a general winding down of superpower confrontations in other parts of the world. This may not be such good news for radical liberation movements, but they were slated for diminishing aid once the Soviet Union began to focus on its own economic problems.

The growing autonomy of Western Europe has been accelerated by the military and economic recklessness of the Reagan administrations on the one hand and by the successful diplomatic peace initiatives by the reformist Gorbachev administration on the other. The Bush administration continues the unpopular American role in Latin America that combines bullying with ineffectiveness in imposing preferred policies. It has shown a complete bankruptcy of imagination and initiative in responding to Soviet peace overtures and the major democratic breakthroughs in Eastern Europe. Thus it has effectively abdicated its role as the political leader of the North Atlantic military alliance and increased the tendency of Western Europeans to assert their own political autonomy and initiative.

A sharp contrast is visible here between the fumbling of the United States and initiatives François Mitterrand took in his role as rotating chair of the European Community in dramatically changing the traditional French attitude toward the prospects of German reunification, or at least rapprochement. The European Community is also showing a far greater readiness to raise large sums immediately to increase the chances of political and economic reforms in Eastern Europe. This again is in sharp contrast with the niggardliness of the U.S. administration, which had to be forced by Congress to increase its miserly offers of help to Poland and Hungary. This growing autonomy in turn raises several specific possibilities: a neutral zone separating Europe from north to south along the lines of the Palme proposal for a nuclear-free zone, or more radically a unified neutral and demilitarized Germany much like contemporary Austria, and a "Finlandized" Eastern Europe in the context of the complete withdrawal by both superpowers of all conventional and nuclear forces from Europe. A German nation of this type could lead the necessary massive reflation of the entire Western European economy through a huge long-range program of exports of goods and technology to the Soviet Union and Eastern Europe. These exports can in turn buy the time necessary for the successful reforms and liberalization of those economies and societies.

An important development for European security, and in fact for security in general, has been the wide and accurate perception among Western military analysts that there is growing acceptance by Soviet military experts of the doctrines of *sufficiency and deterrence*. What this means is that the Soviet deployment of troops and weaponry is consistent with a defensive posture and is less potentially threatening to Western Europe. To be sure, many political observers, myself included, have long argued that for decades no realistic prospect of a war, conventional or nuclear, has existed in Europe. Too much was at stake for both superpowers: neither could risk losing a war in Europe, and a European conflict would necessarily escalate to an all-out worldwide nuclear war. Current Soviet military cutbacks indicate that this reality is formally accepted by at least one superpower. A more reasonable U.S. administration could bring about the acceptance of major reductions by both military establishments as at least not jeopardizing national defense. A beginning of the end of the cold war becomes possible. The lion will not lie down with the lamb, even if it were all that clear which nation is which. But a limited war in Europe with conventional or conventional and "tactical" nuclear weapons will not happen. Even if it did, by some malign miracle, it is not at all clear that NATO as it now stands would not win a smashing victory with the support of the Eastern European populations, who certainly will not fight to defend a system they hate. With the wave of democratic reforms sweeping Eastern Europe the emerging governments will become more popular, but by the same token they will become more European and thus less credible as potential military threats.

The French independent nuclear capacity has in any case guaranteed that no nuclear conflict would be limited to Europe, since once the French responded to an attack with strategic or even so-called intermediate nuclear weapons the fat would be in the fire. In practice they have linked the United States to Western European defense under circumstances in which it is not the United States that unilaterally determines when the conflict goes nuclear. Again, we encounter that capacity that is by no means merely symbolic but actually surpasses in projected number of missiles what Robert McNamara thought was needed *by the United States* to ensure deterrence. The Soviet negotiators led by Gorbachev were intuitively brilliant when they decided to stop insisting on including French and British nuclear weapons in the total when negotiating cutbacks. They understood as few Western analysts—left, right, or center—have understood, namely, that French missiles did not strengthen the United States militarily in Europe but on the contrary made the American presence ultimately unnecessary.

Now if one does not consider there to be a realistic chance of an East-West military conflict in Europe, then nuclear weapons must be looked at in terms of their *political* effect and not their military value, which is nonexistent if war is not anticipated. The political effect of the French nuclear arsenal could be twofold: on the one hand, in the eyes of the traditional pro-Atlanticist elites it makes the French more nearly an equal ally of the United States, replacing West Germany ("rotten with pacifism") as the most reliable ally in the cold war; on the other hand, it builds French confidence that Europe can defend itself without being dependent on the United States. That self-confidence (which leads to greater independence and assertiveness on the part of the European Community) has increased as the Gorbachev peace initiative continues and as it translates into support of liberalizing reforms in Eastern Europe. Self-confidence in this case leads to a maximalist vision of what it is possible to achieve in European unification both in terms of a social Europe and, more important, in terms of who is to be included in that Europe. There is a startling similarity between de Gaulle's vision of a Europe from the Urals to the Atlantic and Gorbachev's talk of a *common European home*. Both metaphors were reassuringly open-ended and vague. However, if Gorbachev's reforms are to have a chance at home he must buy time with diplomatic successes abroad. It is clear that the "soft" Soviet line has been enormously successful in achieving at least three long-range goals of Soviet policy. First, the Soviets have effectively ended the economically ruinous arms race with the United States and NATO. Second, a "soft" Soviet line has done more to weaken NATO's prospects for a prolonged life than all the bluster and threats in the past. And third, democratic reforms, even from above, have made the Soviet Union far more likely to receive major credits and technological aid. Since Eastern European allies have been a drag on the Soviet economy for at least two decades, pushing them out into the world market to fend for themselves with aid from the West will strengthen the Soviet economy.

The inclusion of Hungarian, Polish, and soon East German, Czech, and even Soviet representatives in the European Parliamentary bodies as participant observers is an important step toward a Europe that extend beyond the present EEC. Ironically after all the fears of the cold warriors about the dangers of the Finlandization of West Germany, it is reasonably clear that it is Eastern Europe that will be Finlandized in the very near future. That is, the Eastern European states will be permitted wide autonomy to determine their own forms of government and social and economic policies so long as they respect Soviet security interests. The latter factor may also require some attention to Soviet sensitivities about excessive popular vengeance against the Eastern European Communists once they are out of power. That is why the security interests of the Eastern European states as they grope toward reform and greater autonomy make democracy and tolerance essential. Democracy and tolerance, all too rare in the history of that area, become good common sense and politics. That is not the least important of the gains in *anno mirabilis* 1989 and portends well for European security after 1992.

However, what makes good sense in the long, or even the medium run, is all too rarely the same policy that appears to make sense in the immediate present. Tolerance of differences is essential in order to build stable democratic regimes. It is the precondition for a democratic civic culture. That means no vengeance, no matter how justified, no witch hunts of former Communist hard-liners, and above all no search for scapegoats for what will be economic and social grim times for most of postcommunist Eastern Europe. Those scapegoats will be, all too often, those who are ethnically different, the minorities and Jews. Or they may be the intellectuals or political liberals or leftists.

Eastern Europe is populated with ghosts of chauvinist, populist, and right-wing and corporatist parties. It is important to try to keep these ghosts quiet. Nationalism is the red meat of the organic "genuine" national community, which is all too easy to mobilize against "cool" legal and rational universalism. It is therefore a continual threat to those who would build a multiparty democratic parliamentary legal order. It does not help the prospects for democracy or tolerance that so many of the reformist democratic intellectuals have fallen passionately in love with the idea of the market. For the love of the idea of the market almost as much suffering may be visited on the population of Eastern Europe as had been for the equally abstract idea of centralized planning.

There seems to be no limit to how much suffering can be imposed on the living bodies of existing societies in the name of abstractions. That seems to be the original sin of intellectuals. They have thus set themselves up to be blamed for the grim consequences of their present infatuation with yet another abstraction. In Hungary national populists have already begun attacking "cosmopolitan" (read Jewish) big-city liberals over that precise issue. Similar national populist attacks on economic reforms, and on pluralistic democracy, with or without anti-Semitic subtexts can be expected in Poland, Romania, and the Republic of Serbia in Yugoslavia. The road to democratization runs through perilous straits in Eastern Europe. It has many enemies; few are open, many are covert. They include what remains of the Communist parties and the bureaucrats in the state and other institutions, populists, nationalists, and technocrats. That is why it is essential to help build democratic institutions, trade unions, and civic groups with moral and material aid, which must be supplemented with generous economic and technological aid to these societies. The EEC and EFTA (i.e., Western European democracies) are clearly going to be more generous and effective in providing aid and moral support than the United States.

NOTE

1. "The security of the canal, which matters rather less now than it did 80 years ago, was not at stake; and American interests are unlikely to benefit much from the removal of General Manuel Noriega, who, though corrupt and brutish, posed no threat to regional stability, still less to the United States itself. Instead, Mr. Bush's action in Panama looks like a different kind of intervention: one aimed primarily at public opinion at home" (*The Economist*, Jan. 6-12, 1990, p. 17).

Chapter 2

The Germanys, German Unity, and European Autonomy

The False Stability of the Cold War

For decades the stability of the post-World War II political and frontier settlements in Europe rested on a peculiarly ahistorical assumption of long-range political immobility in the very heart of Europe. I refer to the assumption that the Teheran, Yalta, and Potsdam agreements were set in stone and that no major aspect of their implied division of Europe into two blocs could be altered. To be more accurate, the divisions could not be changed without a major conflict involving the superpowers that were the ultimate guarantors of the stability of a Europe split into two spheres of influence (which were at the same time two sociopolitical systems).

Until the autumn of 1989 it seemed clear to all soberminded observers that no changes in the settlements could be made by peoples who were its objects, the Eastern Europeans who were assigned to the Soviet sphere or the Germans, who were divided into two states. Until the emergence of Gorbachev's more flexible leadership, demonstrations, strikes, and revolts against the division of Europe were spreading, and the imposed communist regimes had to deal not only with their own repressive systems (and the East German regime was certainly efficient in that regard) but also with the near certainty of intervention by the Soviets and other Warsaw Pact members. Massive upheavals therefore seemed suicidal and irresponsible even to the democratic opposition. It was also clear that no substantive aid could be expected from the

West, since such aid would endanger the stable standoff of the super-powers and their alliances.

The new policies in Moscow made possible conditions under which the spontaneous massive pressures from below signaled the entry of the East German people on the scene as an independent subject of politics and history. Nothing will ever be the same again in Germany, Europe, or the world. This may very well disturb many Western observers who, despite their staunch anticommunism, were content to accept *as desirable* the division of Germany, and as inevitable if sad, the subjection of Eastern Europe. In the eyes of some, both were being justly punished for the past sins of their nation and region, perhaps for centuries of anti-Semitism and for the failure, with the exception of Czechoslovakia, to develop a genuinely democratic political tradition. It was another case of blaming the victim.

That is why after the initial euphoria among American and Western European leaders wears off, and that will be very quickly indeed, a host of unanticipated problems will surface. After all, most of the democratic oratory was for the public; it was meant to score well-deserved points against the Communist authoritarians. It was not meant to be taken all that seriously, and above all it was not supposed to happen on one's watch so that one would have to do something in response. For example, will the West respond to freedom of travel for Eastern Europeans and Soviet citizens by opening up immigration, or will it raise other walls, barriers just as real if less visible and ugly than the one that just went down in Berlin. If the Soviet Union withdraws all troops from Eastern Europe, will the United States do the same in Western Europe? The revolutionary transformation of Eastern Europe opens a Pandora's box of issues.

At the heart of that division, and symbolizing it in its most intense form, was the division of Germany into two states representing two rival social, economic, and political systems. The two Germanys were the showpieces of their respective systems, as well as the focal points of the two military alliances, NATO and the Warsaw Pact. Both were the site of the largest concentration of armed might of the two rival alliances. Both were obviously designated as the central battlefield if armed conflict were to break out. Further, and by no means less significantly, *neither* had the ability to determine when, under what circumstances, and with what weapons, conventional or nuclear war would be fought on their soil. Neither controlled the vast nuclear arsenals stationed within their borders. And lastly, each was the strongest and most reliable economic and military ally of its own superpower. All that would not have seemed to be a recipe for long-range stability, since it ran against the most basic yearnings for self-determination, national independence, and even survival.

Ultimately, however, the stability of the division of Europe and Germany rested on two further assumptions, the first being that, whatever the reforms and changes within individual members of the two alliances, the *fundamental* socioeconomic and political systems would remain stable. That guarantee was implicit in the West and made explicit in Eastern Europe in the form of the Brezhnev Doctrine. The second assumption was so taken for granted that it never had to be spelled out. It was that the cold war was a more or less permanent state of affairs; that is, it could intensify or simmer down, but it would remain the permanent state of relations between the two alliances in Europe.

A First Warning:
The Austrian Peace Treaty of 1955

The only significant exception to the rule about the irreversibility of communist regimes and the borders between them and the West, and one that should have been a more general warning about similar future possibilities on the larger scale which Germany afforded, was the Austrian Peace Treaty signed in 1955. It was the *only* example, until 1989, of a voluntary withdrawal of Soviet power in Europe and the abandonment of a faithful local communist regime since World War II.[1] In 1989 the rules seemed to change, and it became increasingly obvious that the Soviets *were* willing to abandon faithful clients within the Eastern European states. To say that the Soviets were "willing" is to understate the case; they clearly pushed toward reforms and an opening up in at least two countries, East Germany and Czechoslovakia. No change was imaginable in Bulgaria, the most faithful of allies, without Soviet blessing. It also became clear that the Soviets were willing to put up with governments in which the Communist party no longer had a leading role.

What remains interesting about the Austrian treaty as a historical precedent were the terms of the trade-off: unity within a Western-style political democracy in exchange for Austrian neutrality and a permanent prohibition of its participation in alliances. Under those circumstances Soviet troops withdrew from their occupation zone of Austria and left the Austrian Communists to the tender mercies of free elections. The result was predictable: almost overnight the Austrian Communist party became for all intents and purposes a sect. The bar to participation in any alliance, initially absolute, was finally modified under

Gorbachev's leadership in the late 1980s to permit Austria to apply for membership in the EEC, another most significant precedent. I suspect that historical reexaminations of the Austrian Peace Treaty will become the subject of a minor boom. Those reexaminations can raise a whole host of interesting questions about what might have been, how Central Europe might have evolved, if the United States and its allies had not been so intent on integrating West Germany into their alliance. Could it be that the division of Germany into two states and social systems had been avoidable as early as the 1950s?

In turn, other interesting revisions of history and evaluations of historical responsibility will probably take place. For example, was the creation of the Eastern European bloc of Soviet satellites in the late 1940s and early 1950s the result of a long-range Soviet plan, or did it develop haphazardly? Did the Soviets acquire an empire through a combination of reactions to real or perceived Western (i.e., U.S.) moves, and to unanticipated opportunities and openings afforded by the clumsiness and narrowness of the Eastern European non-Communists? Were those endless dreary decades of repression and stagnation a historical accident? Was it perhaps an unnecessary suffering imposed on the mass of Eastern Europeans by a mixture of incompetence, misunderstanding, and the usual lack of firmness on the part of Western powers when it came to defending *democracy* as distinct from spheres of influence? This was fatally combined with a brutal and crude communism at its dogmatic worst in Stalin's last years. Was "Finlandization" an option even then? We will of course never know. Nevertheless there were many signs that the stability of the Eastern European settlements was fragile and would require considerable outside force to maintain. Constant revolts and disturbances in East Germany in 1951, the repeated turbulence in Poland, the Hungarian revolt of 1956, the Prague spring of 1968, and the growth in Poland of Solidarity, the largest mass workers' movement in Europe, were the rumblings of a volcano. Trying to keep the lid on forever seems now to have been a futile effort to preserve a negative and doomed utopia.

Prior to the events of 1989, however, very few observers, scholars, politicians, and journalists argued that Eastern Europe would not remain stable under Communist-run dictatorships and that German reunification could not be kept forever off the political agenda. I will immodestly claim that I was a minor exception to this generalization, and in several articles in the journal *Dissent* and in public lectures, I contended that German reunification would soon become the unavoidable political issue in Europe. I also claimed that labor turbulence, pressures from below, would be the nemesis of the Eastern European politocracies. That claim, which was at least in part correct, is argued at some length in *The Limits of Change*. However gratifying it may be to be an exception to the rule that Western social scientists and political analysts were for the most part wrong in their estimate of the future of German reunification and Eastern Europe, the real question is why most analysts were wrong, not why very few were right. Part of the answer is that most were mesmerized by the cold war and would not or could not imagine its termination. Too much of the stability of the postwar settlements seemed to be at stake. One's conception of the role of both the United States *and* the Soviet Union—one's entire worldview—would have to change. Academies are after all profoundly conservative institutions and the media are not known to be havens of innovative thought.

Entire generations of political analysts have been brought up with a fixed, and reassuringly consistent, picture of the necessary enemy, an aggressively expanding world communism under the leadership of the Soviet Union. To believe that these were decrepit and stagnant states with little or no support from their populations would have been to downplay the danger and to make the arms race and the cold war absurd. To argue further, as a few of us did, that the Warsaw Pact was fatally weak because the people of Eastern Europe would not fight to defend the regimes they hated was to attack the rationale behind the massive arms buildup by the United States that began in the last years of the Carter administration and accelerated under Reagan. It meant to oppose the pressure on the Western European nations to increase military spending.

While it was not necessary that one have any illusions about the nature of the authoritarian regime in the Soviet Union or about its international benevolence, one did have to consider the massive U.S. arms buildup as a reckless and unnecessary endangerment of world peace. In short, one had to consider *both* superpowers as a problem: both jeopardized world peace, and both imposed unpopular regimes where they found it served their interests to do so. In short, the interest of European independence and peace requires independence from both superpowers.

Recent historical changes in Eastern Europe, including the dramatic and spontaneous entrance on the scene of the people of East Germany as an independent political actor who toppled the repressive Honecker regime and forced the destruction of the hated Berlin Wall, mark the end of that stability. The successful and wide-ranging Gorbachev peace initiatives and the Soviet agreement to the installation of a Solidarity-dominated, noncommunist government in Warsaw put the future of the cold war itself in question. A hostile, armed, and potentially threatening Warsaw Pact is being replaced by an alliance that has adopted a clearly defensive posture and insists on its commitment to democratizing reforms.

The Soviets and their allies have been sharply cutting back on armaments and reducing the number of Soviet troops stationed in Eastern Europe, in some cases unilaterally. They have extricated themselves from the quagmire of Afghanistan, where for years they had seemed determined to show that they were incapable of learning from the lessons of the American defeat in Vietnam. Instead of being a barrier to liberalizing reforms in Eastern Europe they are now actively promoting them, even, or perhaps especially, at the cost of removing a whole generation of faithful but unpopular timeservers in those regimes. Far from menacing it, they now petition Western Europe for financial and economic aid with which to begin rebuilding economies ravaged by decades of mismanagement. Not only does a general detente in Europe therefore seem very much a prospect, but the Soviet leader also talks in terms of a common European home. Gorbachev pursues this brilliant metaphor in his book *Perestroika* by pointing out that in this common European home there will be many rooms, which presumably will not be identical, and there will also be several entrances. Be that as it may, it is a very different Soviet leadership that now faces Europe. It is also a leadership that has gone a long way to court the Federal Republic of Germany as the most obvious source of credit and technology for the ailing Soviet economy. This leadership is also in good part responsible for the bloodless victory of the reformist current in the East German Communist leadership. It is also clear that events took on a life of their own and the communist rule began unraveling far more rapidly than the Soviets expected.

German Reunification: Back on the Agenda

Any prospect of a general detente in Europe reopens the long-dormant "German question" (that is, the reunification or coming together of the two Germanys). Historically, it is primarily the United States and its allies that are responsible for the existence of a divided Germany. For decades the tacit assumption has been that European, particularly Western European, stability depended on a weak Germany. As a French politician put it, "We love Germany so much that we prefer to see at least two of them." The division of Germany against the wishes of the German people, no matter how convenient for some, was and remains a gross violation of the most elementary right of self-determination. The continuation of this violation depends either on sterile neo-Machiavellian politics, which assume that popular will is a mere inconvenience for serious politics, or on the premise that collective national guilt justifies punishing generations of Germans who were not even born when the Nazis were in power. It is a not-so-minor scandal that many democratic politicians of Western Europe have remained comfortable with this ongoing violation of national rights in the very heart of Europe. It was one thing to say that the Yalta and Potsdam settlements could not be challenged by force of arms; it was quite another to rationalize the division of Germany as serving some higher good other than the mere will of the people involved. Among the most vociferous rationalizers of the continued division of Germany were the Communists and their sympathizers, who were equally ready to defend the armed unification of Korea or Vietnam.

The Soviets, under Stalin in the early 1950s, had shown an almost indecent willingness to sacrifice their East German party loyalists in their desire to achieve an Austrian-style settlement in Germany. This deal for a unified but demilitarized and neutral Germany, exactly like today's Austria, has been offered repeatedly and is the nightmare of the supporters of NATO and of the notion that the cold war must last forever. How could one even imagine a NATO without West Germany, which provides half the ground forces as well as the actual terrain on which a conflict would be fought? What if the danger of military conflict in Europe is reduced to the vanishing point? Why would the West and East German peoples agree to a continued and artificial separation in the name of nonexistent security considerations? It is to the immense credit of François Mitterrand that he was the first Western European leader to revise the traditional French support for a continued division of Germany and advocate the eventual reunification of the two German states within a unified Europe.

Although it is likely that in the most immediate future radical democratic reforms in East Germany and a gradual economic integration of the two Germanys, rather than any unification or joint federal state, will be on the agenda, that is only a long step in the direction of further integration and eventual reunification. Steps toward a confederation of the two German states will probably be taken in the near future. The political, economic, and social *content* of that confederation will depend on many circumstances, not the least of which will be the speed with which democratic reforms are adopted in East Germany and the strength of continued pressure from below for change. My own view is that a host of trans-German ties will begin to develop to supplement the agreed upon economic ones. For example, the small *East* German Social Democratic

party, once formally legalized, can be counted on to develop close organizational ties with the West German Social Democratic party. The
larger Social Democratic party of the Federal Republc will certainly aid,
as it has already begun aiding, its East German sister party. It would be
grotesque if it did not, since it has assisted other fledgling social democratic movements and parties throughout the world. A whole network
of relations, including close cooperation between the two youth organizations, joint seminars, and conferences and activities, will grow. The
same is the case with the Green party, the peace movement, and many
other organizations.

Two trans-German links will be of considerable importance. It is
reasonable to expect the unification of the Lutheran and Catholic
churches to anticipate formal development of a federal or confederal
state. It is even more certain that very close cooperation, perhaps even
de facto merger, will take place between the West German trade unions
and the much reformed new genuine East German unions. One possible model is the long-standing relationship between American and
Canadian unions. A number of them are organizationally unified although there is often a separate Canadian regional organization. Fur-
thermore, the Canadian region has a different set of political ties from
the ones that exist in the United States, since the labor social democratic party in Canada, the New Democratic party, has no equivalent in
the United States. In the same way one can visualize a unified German
trade union movement that has somewhat different political systems to
deal with in the two Germanys. That they will start cooperating very
closely indeed is, however, certain. It is a case of pure and pressing self-
interest. The West German unions cannot welcome massive government
and private investment from the Federal Republic and job creation in an
East Germany where wages and conditions are markedly below West
German standards. The obvious way to combat that problem is to help
the East German unions develop standards close to those of the Western
ones as quickly as possible. It also means to work for common laws concerning safety, working conditions, social security, and the rest.

Much of this can be done under the aegis of common rules of the
European Community, of which East Germany becomes a de facto part
through its special relationship with the Federal Republic. Whether
through the EEC rules or joint intra-German coordination, a whole set
of legal and institutional ties will be developed — common policy on education, common administration of transport, expansion of cooperation on criminal legislation and law enforcement, and so on. In the near
future one can expect that passports will be abolished between the two
German states and that citizens will be able to travel back and forth with

their standard identity cards. Increased communication and travel will make excessive differences in prices of goods and services intolerable. Then there is West German farming legislation with its many subsidies, which must necessarily be attractive to long-suffering East German farmers. The list is endless and it will begin to expand in the immediate future.

The old seductive Austrianization deal, the Rapacki Plan of the early 1950s, and versions of the Palme proposals all advocated essentially the same thing: a block of neutral states starting with Sweden in the north and moving through the Germanys to Austria, then on to Yugoslavia and Albania. Such a step would have a number of heuristic side effects, two of them being that it would deal near-fatal blows to both NATO and the Warsaw Pact, and it would be likely to spread the zone both eastward and westward—Czechoslovakia, Hungary, and Poland on the one hand being obvious candidates, and Denmark, Norway, and the Benelux countries on the other.[2] Such a zone gives more solid security guarantees to the Soviet Union than does a Warsaw Pact based on an alliance with regimes detested by their populations.

One can probably say that the Soviet Union was never more popular in Eastern Europe or Germany than it is now, when it appears least threatening and most committed to wide-ranging reforms. Rather than being presented with a group of reformed communist governments that might in some cases include a few non-Communists, the Soviets will face an Eastern Europe that has changed dramatically. Liberal reformers never seem to learn that, unlike reforms from above, revolutions from below are impossible to fine-tune. This is particularly true where spontaneous and unorganized entry of the population into politics has occurred, rather than protracted negotiations with an organized opposition that has wide legitimacy. Where organized democratic forces exist, the gains made through turbulence from below can be used to form stable new institutional settlements. Where experienced democratic opposition is not established, the prospects for a transition to stable democratic regimes are much more problematic.

The temptation to resort to nationalistic, enthnocentric, and populist pseudoegalitarian demagoguery will be great and it will pay off in the short run. In some cases that demagoguery will be the instrument wielded by what remains of the communist *nomenklaturas*, institutions, and cadres within the bureaucracies as well as in the political process, as a way of holding on to power. This is particularly true when there has as yet not been enough time to develop genuinely broadly based programmatic political parties and movements to fill the political void created by the collapse of the Communist parties as credible political organizations. It would have been wildly utopian to expect that years of grim repression under communist regimes had left behind a mass political culture that was in its essence democratic and tolerant. The values of democratic and human rights activists have been relatively ghettoized to the better-educated publics in much of this region. It is important not to assume that the massive turning against the communist regimes was and is programmatically inspired by the politics and values of oppositional activists. That opposition was and is far broader and includes a visceral and massive anticommunism that has precious little in common with democratic values.

The postcommunist politics of Eastern Europe will in many ways resemble Mexico, with all the present ambiguities of corporatism, corruption, a dynamic private sector, and a multitude of political parties, most of which have no effective access to power or broad support. One must not push the analogy too far, but it is richly suggestive. These will also be societies where the role of international financial institutions and banks will be important as well as a source of great internal hostility and controversy. These are a part of the historical penalty being paid by these societies for the lost years under communist regimes. To aid the prospects of genuine democracy in the region, political, economic, and moral pressure from the Western European advocates of democracy, Social Democratics, and trade unionists can make a difference. It must be made clear that the quantity and type of aid, not to mention the relationship to the European Community, will depend on the degree to which the Eastern European states abide by democratic norms and respect human rights, and that this explicitly includes independent trade unions and social movements. For that pressure to have any real effect, the international financial institutions must not be permitted to continue to demand policies that impose a brutal austerity difficult for any democratic or popular regime to survive. The trouble is that economists all too often ignore the social and political consequences of their proposals. Sensible people must insist that, outside of economic models and college classrooms, there is no such thing as a "purely" economic policy that can be isolated from social and political consequences.

Social Democrats and German Unity

One of the precursors of the process now moving the two Germanys toward some kind of reunification was clearly the *Ostpolitik* or Eastern policy initiated by Willy Brandt when he headed the Social Democratic government in the Federal Republic. Brandt's was a soft and conciliatory

approach that reassured West Germany's eastern neighbors and at-
tempted to normalize relations with the East German government, and
it slowly but surely produced results. West Germany developed ever
more numerous bilateral arrangements throughout the area, thereby expanding its economic influence and ability to intervene on behalf of the
German minorities. The more autonomous the foreign policy of West
Germany from that of the United States, the greater its leverage in Eastern Europe and with the Soviet Union.

The West German Social Democrats have also been pushed steadily
to the left by the relentless hostility of Washington under Ronald Reagan
on the one hand and by pressure from the Greens and other new social
movements on the other. All this makes one wonder just how long it will
take for the Social Democrats to link the campaign for German reunification on a democratic and peace-strengthening basis with the old Austrian model and the call for the Finlandization of Eastern Europe. The
Social Democrats have many reasons to push for speedy reunification,
and happily principle and expediency seem to come together here.
Clearly no democratically minded person, let alone a Democratic Socialist, can do anything but support the democratic right of the two German peoples to unite if they so desire—that is, if they express that desire through democratically elected parliaments and/or referenda. It is
simply a matter of principle. However, and happily for the Social Democrats, in this case virtue is rewarded, since all indications are that
whereas the Communists would get between 6 percent and 8 percent of
the vote in a free East German election, the Social Democrats would win
handily. This is because a large part of the East German public accepts
a "socialism with a human face," that is, a socialism with a mixed economy, an advanced welfare state, and political democracy. In other words,
some—amazingly enough—like the program of the Social Democrats.
Here it is also useful to remember that the present East Germany includes the traditional electoral strongholds of the left. Because the Communists have discredited themselves with the electorate, that left vote
would go to the Social Democrats and to a lesser extent to the Greens.
That is reasonably clear from the statement of various oppositional
groups in East Germany today.

The Social Democrats have two other major advantages compared
to the other West German parties on the political terrain of East Germany. The first is the probability that the reformed trade unions in East
Germany will start developing close ties with West German unions. This
is not only for purposes of seeking support and aid in developing modern trade unions, which is readily available, but even more to develop
joint strategies for dealing with private capital as it begins to invest in

East Germany. Neither West nor East German trade unions will accept a semicolonial relationship in which cheap East German labor is used to attack trade union gains and standards in West Germany. That is why close, practical, and unsentimental ties between the trade unions in the two Germanys are needed. This relationship can foreshadow similar relationships with reformed trade unions in Hungary, Yugoslavia, Czechoslovakia, and Poland. And this where the Social Democrats, in their close link to the unions, have an edge over the bourgeois parties.

Germany can almost certainly unify and still be able to stay in the European Community, since the Soviets have raised no objections to Austria's current moves in that direction. In any case, East Germany has had a peculiar halfway house relationship to the community for years. I can imagine few more powerful electoral planks for the Social Democrats in West Germany than to call for a unified democratic Germany in an independent and peaceful Europe. These trends have been encouraged by the development of a Soviet diplomatic program that is increasingly successful in projecting the image of a Soviet Union that genuinely needs, for its own economic and technological reasons, truly massive reductions in military expenditures and a prolonged detente.

By the same token those who would interfere with the three desiderata of West German policy will not be the bearers of welcome tidings. The three propositions are: no increase in military spending or numbers of troops, an expansion and deepening of the special relationship between the Germanys, and an expansion of long-range trade and access to raw materials and markets in the East. Following the upheavals of 1989, to these are added two more policy imperatives for the West German stance toward East Germany. The first is support for basic democratic reforms, including free elections, free trade unions, and freedom of political organization as a precondition for truly massive aid and investments in the East Germany economy. Only this can prevent East German mass migration now that travel restrictions have been lifted. The effect would of course be to make the two Germanys a good deal more alike than they are now. The second is to support steps, no matter how gradual and cautious they are, for the reunification of the two German states.

Let me emphasize that I refer here not to the integration of East Germany into the Federal Republic of Germany but to integration leading to some kind of federation of the *two Germanys*. It should be reasonably clear that while German unification and measures making life more tolerable for their cousins in the German Democratic Republic are broadly popular in West Germany, the immediate political beneficiaries of any of these measures will be the Social Democrats, for all sorts of obvious and not so obvious reasons.

Some Problems and Dangers in German Unification

Other political consequences of a drawing closer of the two Germanys are not necessarily so benign. One consequence of the de facto opening of the frontiers between the two states will be the continual pressure of illegal immigration via East Germany into the Federal Republic. Already hundreds of thousands of Polish citizens have applied for guest worker status in East Germany. To be sure, many will be satisfied to work for East German wages, which will be higher than Polish wages for some time. There have been guest workers from other communist states, including Vietnam, and this could soon become a major problem. In fact, the growing integration of the two economies will press East German wages upward and probably make the East German mark a convertible currency in the near future. Nevertheless, while many will be content to remain in East Germany as guest workers, many others will be tempted to cross the ever more open border into West Germany.

Two consequences will follow from these circumstances. The first is already present; namely, it will become increasingly difficult for Poles, and by inference Hungarians and other Eastern Europeans, to claim political asylum. That is not even particularly unfair, since the vast majority of the current immigrants from Eastern Europe and the Soviet Union, including Soviet Jews, are *not* political refugees in any meaningful sense. They find their societies unpleasant, drab, and lacking in economic opportunities. This is true of millions of people around the world and does not serve to mobilize much support and solidarity from the host nation. One consequence is that the immigrants who are seeking entry are not only from Eastern Europe and Turkey, which after all are peripheries of Europe, but increasingly from Bangladesh, Africa, the Middle East, Latin America, the Philippines, and Asia. Various catastrophes, human-made and otherwise, will only increase this pressure, particularly if Europe appears as one of the few islands of prosperity, stability, and peace in a world foundering in economic, ecological, and political crises. The second consequence will be the all but inevitable growth of nationalist and anti-immigrant parties of the right in Germany and in the rest of Europe.

The growth of the right-wing Republicans in the Federal Republic (particularly in West Berlin) and of Le Pen's rightists in France is a harbinger of things to come. Anti-immigrant and anticosmopolitan nationalism is a natural and ugly response to the expanding integration of Europe and the integration of that Europe into the world economy. It is important to stress here that anti-immigrant sentiments and right-wing nationalism are not at all specifically German problems. They are also widespread in France, Belgium, Austria, Denmark, and Great Britain. One can even argue that German society is somewhat better inoculated against the virus of racism and neofascism than many other parts of Europe, East or West. The more reassuring argument, however, lies in the nature of the present dominant left in West Germany. The left does not suffer from the type of debilitating split that crippled it in confronting Hitler in 1933; the Communists are now completely marginal in West German politics, and their popularity in East Germany has weakened. The German Social Democrats are completely hegemonic on the left, and staunchly democratic. Unlike the German Communists in 1933, who argued that social democracy was merely another form of fascism and that bourgeois democracy was no better than fascism, the vast majority of the left in Germany today firmly defend democracy. Even most of the bourgeois parties in West Germany are at least as committed to the defense of democracy as are their counterparts in the rest of Europe. If there is any ambivalence in this formulation it is because the Federal Republic was heavy-handed beyond what Social Democrats could tolerate in dealing with the Red Brigades and the country's minuscule Communist party. Nevertheless a whole new generation has grown up and been educated to appreciate both democracy and a wider, more cosmopolitan worldview than their parents and grandparents had.

The youth culture of young Germans has for decades been the despair of nationalists and traditionalists. It is happily far too individualistic and resistant to authority. It is startlingly similar to that wellspring of international youth culture, that of the United States. Whatever else one thinks about this transnational culture, it is, with few exceptions, essentially antiauthoritarian and antiracist. Those exceptions are also rooted in an antibourgeois worldview (if something so serious can be ascribed to it), but this alternate view does have similarities to the forms of nihilism and despair that spawned the intellectual currents of fascism in the 1920s. These currents, however, are stronger in Great Britain and France than in Germany, and it is an open question how much they represent a playing with the forbidden fruit the young find so attractive. In any case, given how very different contemporary young Germans are from the prewar generations, fears about the growth of a massive right in Germany seem misplaced. It can only be based on theories of a national character seen as inherent, rather than socially formed. This is but a rehashing of the old nature versus nurture argument, and I for one believe that political cultures are not biologically based but are products of human agency.

Thus while I foresee a moderate growth of right-wing politics in Germany in the face of an increasingly cosmopolitan Germany within an increasingly cosmopolitan and less "Eurocentric" Europe, I think this will be within the range of such developments throughout the European community. It is simply impossible to keep denying the Germans the right to national unification and self-determination on the basis of supposed collective national guilt and ineradicable national character.

Here one could only add that while the monstrous crimes of Nazi Germany can never be compensated for, West Germany almost uniquely among modern nations did acknowledge responsibility and did attempt to make some restitution to the victims of its predecessor regime. To date the German Democratic Republic has failed to do so. For that matter the United States has not compensated Vietnam, or the Central and Latin American countries it has oppressed. Britain, France, Belgium, Italy, and Holland have failed to compensate their colonies. The Israelis have done nothing for the innocent Palestinian civilian victims of their settlement programs, nor has the Soviet Union proposed to compensate the victims of its gulags. And the litany goes on. For that matter the *other* perpetrators of anti-Semitic mass slaughters in Romania, Slovakia, Vichy France, the Ukraine, and Hungary were not followed by governments that acknowleged at least some responsibility and offered some, no matter how symbolic, compensation. I mention this to stress that it is not possible to keep insisting on the perpetual special guilt of Germany without violating the rights of present and future generations of Germans.

NOTES

1. The only other example I can think of was the withdrawal of Soviet troops and the collapse of a pro-Soviet regime in northern Iran at the end of World War II. One could also stretch it to put forth Finland as an example of voluntary withdrawal of Soviet military presence.

2. Free elections for the federal Parliament in a unified Germany would almost certainly produce a near-permanent Social Democratic majority. This trade between the Soviet Union and a unified Germany is even more likely, since the chances of political strings being attached to such a trade would be minimized.

Chapter 3

The End of an Empire:
Eastern Europe and the Soviet Union

The dramatic upheavals in Eastern Europe resulting both from mass democratic pressures from below and long-overdue reforms and liberalization from above highlight the general crisis of the state "socialist" systems ruled by Communist parties.[1] Gorbachev's acceptance of the desperate urgency for fundamental political and economic reforms has begun to transform the Soviet and Eastern European state socialist systems. To put it more precisely the reforms Gorbachev needs require a different international setting, a winding down of the cold war, and this has as a precondition the liberalization and opening up of the Eastern European state "socialist" politocracies. This precondition calls for radically altering Soviet expectations for what the regimes in Eastern Europe must conform to, and that in turn permits reforms that were unimaginable before 1989. The very speed with which the changes are occurring creates special and unprecedented problems. For example, the deposing of ruling Communist parties creates an institutional vacuum; in most of the countries, with the exception of Poland, the opposition was small, loosely organized, and relatively isolated. It takes time and effective communication to build alternative parties and institutions, and the whole point of repression was to stifle the ties of minimal social solidarity and mutual confidence, thus preventing a massive democratic opposition from emerging. The ruling parties had been partially successful in crippling the opposition. It remained small and ghettoized until it was catapulted, ready or not, into responsibility and the political limelight by mass popular demonstrations. The model of the democratic revolutions in Czechoslovakia and East Germany followed not Lenin's scenario but Rosa Luxemburg's—that is, mass spon-

45

taneous eruption from below rather than careful tactics and strategy by a self-selected revolutionary general staff, a cadre leading disciplined troops. While such movements succeeded admirably in toppling the evidently illegitimate authority of the communist regimes, building alternative legitimate democratic authority is a very difficult task. It will be made ever more difficult by the presence of marginal groups of defeated Communist hard-liners on the one hand and right-wing nationalistic adventurers on the other, antagonists who share a goal, preventing the stabilization of a democratic order through provocations, riots, and violence if necessary. After all, the CIA and KGB do not have a monopoly on the scenario for destabilizing democratic regimes; there can be other less established players.

The spontaneous mass upsurges from below were and remain essentially unorganized; they did not enhance the organizational strength of the opposition groups and movements. These groups will therefore have great difficulty in presenting well-formulated platforms for alternative policies and in developing candidates with adequate visibility and legitimacy to form new governments. But the old ruling parties have clearly lost what dubious legitimacy they had, and this creates a vacuum of legitimate authority needed to administer a modern state. This is all the more painful since these countries face the need for profound and quite stressful and difficult economic and political reforms that are hard to carry out in the best of circumstances; the institutional vacuum and absence of broadly legitimate authority make this virtually impossible.

Historically both the horrendous backlog of reforms and the institutional void are the responsibility of the ruling Communist parties. That is why those parties will pay a heavy political penalty in any democratic competitive system; that does not help the alternate movements and opposition, however. These movements had learned to oppose and criticize; often they were focused on a single issue; usually their membership was limited to intellectuals. Now they have the more complicated task of learning how to offer alternative national policies for which they will have to take political responsibility. They will have to learn how to compromise with stubborn reality, make coalitions with difficult partners, and administer complex and deeply troubled societies. In short, they will have to learn democracy, that same democracy for which they fought for so many hopeless years. They will find that a hard task, perhaps even an impossible one without generous help from Western Europe and the United States.

What Do These Societies Have in Common?

Any analysis of the crisis of the Soviet Union and Eastern Europe must necessarily begin with the question of the similarities of those political, economic, and social orders to each other—in other words, their common character, if there is one. I believe the best way to describe these systems is as *politocracies*, that is, systems in which the political elites, ruling usually but exclusively through the Communist party, control the state and the economy, and as a result the society.

Elsewhere I discuss my present preference for the term "politocracy" to describe societies diversely known as state socialist or currently existing socialisms or authoritarian socialism.[2] The term is borrowed with gratitude from the well-known Yugoslav political theorist Svetozar Stojanović. I think its explanatory power is superior to the other attempts to describe the system that emerged after the isolation of the Bolshevik revolution and the counterrevolution led by Stalin in 1929-30 created an unprecedented new social and political order in the Soviet Union.

The same system was imposed after World War II on those parts of Eastern Europe assigned to the Soviet sphere of influence. I do not regard these regimes as any variant of socialism; on the contrary, they have become for the vast majority of people the paradigm of what is wrong with socialism. All basic economic reforms of these systems must have as their essential precondition the destruction of stubbornly entrenched privilege and the monopoly on political power that are primarily those of the politocracy and their families and allies. Those have been maintained by the monopoly on power the Communist parties have had in these countries. All reforms must therefore begin by destroying that monopoly. No lasting economic reforms, no liberalization of the political systems have any long-range prospects without that first step. That is not to say that no reforms are possible that would represent major improvements in the way these societies function without eliminating the legal and very real monopoly on power the Communist parties in those societies possess. What I am asserting is that no lasting basic economic and political reforms, which are essential if the present crisis of these societies is to be resolved, are possible so long as that monopoly is maintained. This is true for a number of reasons, the fundamental one being that this monopoly cannot be maintained without constant violation of democracy and the right of people to organize their own parties, unions, movements, and institutions. That is, one cannot begin to develop a civil society, which is a necessary companion to democracy. Without minimal social autonomy from the party and state one also cannot have any genuine economic reforms, since they will always be subordinated to the political intervention and will of the party.

Examining contemporary Eastern European societies, all the differences in their paths of reforms and democratization notwithstanding, permits us to speculate within limits about the future of at least some of the reforms proposed in the Soviet Union. They are moreover a barometer for what the Soviets will accept as being within the range of permissible change. Examining Eastern Europe today also permits us to speculate about a more general question: what are the general limits and possibilities of change in the comunist regimes? A number of the currently proposed Soviet reforms, or others essentially similar in conception, have been experimented with for over two decades on the much smaller scale of the individual Eastern European countries. Political changes far more radical than any now proposed in the Soviet Union are taking place in Eastern Europe, and their failure or success will help determine the future Soviet agenda.

Comparisons must be made with great caution, since the Eastern European communist regimes have been imposed by the Soviet Union on those countries and have had the double burden of being responsible for enforcing unpopular policies *and* instruments for continued Soviet domination. The German Democratic Republic also has a unique problem posed by the very existence of the Federal Republic, which is in almost every way the more successful of the two Germanys. Nevertheless there are sufficient similarities for Eastern Europe to be at least a cracked mirror of the Soviet Union's possible future, or in any case the most probable future.

It is true, however, that after four decades of communist rule the Eastern European states developed in nationally specific directions. The politocratic regimes were after all *imposed* on societies with a wide range of economic developments, cultural traditions, and political histories. This has made for increasingly "national" variants of communism even within the Warsaw Pact bloc. Extreme national variants, like those in Albania and Yugoslavia, led to breaks with the bloc decades ago. These differences will increase as these societies move further into economic and political reforms that will if anything accent the nationally specific character of each country within the bloc.

The gap in economic and political performance between the individual states will steadily increase. Some states will delay the introduction of democratic reforms for some time. In others the Communist parties will, formally or informally, maintain some level of authority and power. They do begin with the advantage of resources and organization, but the question is how much weight this carries in the face of widespread contempt and even hatred on the part of the population. Then what happens if, as will inevitably happen in some cases, the new democratic governments stumble, plunging the country into major economic uncertainty and chaos? This is not at all far-fetched given the attitude of Western banks and creditors on the one hand and illusions about the magical workings of the market on the other. What happens when the bad old days of communist regimes become remembered as the good old days of stability and security? Democracy is a hard-won thing, the fledgling democracies will desperately need massive and generous help. In still other cases there will be coalitions with right-wing nationalist and populist forces. Some will evolve into democratic polities that are no longer politocracies.

It is difficult to describe these new social and political hybrids, since real societies do not neatly fall into categories such as "socialist" and "capitalist." It is hard, for example, to imagine a "capitalism" without real capitalists, and I believe that all the talk about privatizing the public sector of the economy and moving into a market-driven economic system notwithstanding, the reality will be much more complicated. For one thing, certain essential infrastructures will be impossible to privatize. For another, much of the public sector is not going to be all that attractive to potential buyers. These will be transitional societies with a mixture of institutional and economic forms, with a *variety* of forms of ownership, public, state, cooperative, private, and a mix of all these. I agree with Alec Nove's argument that such a mix is desirable and sensible. Whether this makes such a society "socialist" or "capitalist" is a problem of definition. My own rough answer is that this will depend on the *specific* balance of organized political and class forces as well as on the specific mix of forms of ownership in the society. This will also be complicated by the degree of state intervention, through direct and indirect mechanisms, in attempting to do some planning, which after all differs so greatly in clearly capitalist economies. Obviously these societies will develop genuine trade unions and democratic Socialist parties, under whatever name as well. Whatever else is the case, the struggle for socialism will be a great deal easier in Eastern Europe once these societies democratize.

What happens in Eastern Europe and the Soviet Union has a direct bearing on the future prospects of socialist politics anywhere in the world, since the repressive realities of communist dictatorships that had defined themselves as socialist have helped put the very idea of socialism in question everywhere. Whatever democratic Socialists may say about these societies not having been genuine socialist societies, those experiences do bear on the validity of at least some major assumptions shared by Socialists in general. At the very least they cast a negative light on the performance of centralized command economies at other than early industrialization stages of development. The very existence of a model of authoritarian socialism was a major burden for Socialists in countries with a democratic tradition and institutions. It created a constant need to differentiate from that type of authoritarian socialism. It also did untold damage to the very term socialism in Eastern Europe and the Soviet Union. Quite simply for most of the population, if what those systems represented was socialism, they were, with absolute justification, against it.

Both the realities and fantasies about these systems, which had defined themselves and were widely accepted as some variants of socialism, were something for which some kind of intellectual and above all moral responsibility was laid at the door of socialism itself, as a project and a worldview. This is in good part because to this very day a number of Western Marxists or Socialists continue to refer to these societies as socialist, although nowadays it is usually euphemistically as "currently existing socialism" or simply as "state socialism."

What I believe is that today these societies have similar class and political structures and an essentially similar class in power. I now believe, however, that politocracies can have a wide range of possible political forms with more or less autonomy for independent organizations and trade unions and more or less political rights and individual liberty, just like the more familiar bourgeois societies. The *content* of those societies in terms of real rights and freedoms will be determined by the balance of social and political forces.

The Soviet Union at the end of the 1980s had become a force for change rather than an obstacle to reforms in these societies. This removed what had been the most important barrier to democratic reforms in Eastern Europe. However, this necessary condition for change in the Eastern European states is clearly not sufficient. Indeed, the crucial difference is the appearance of mass pressure from below. The strength of this pressure, whether organized as in the case of Solidarity in Poland, spontaneous as in East Germany and Czechoslovakia, or even mostly latent as in Hungary, determines both the success and the range of democratic reforms. What can be given from above can also be taken back. Change won through struggle establishes new power relations. Further, the fate of democratic reforms ultimately rests on the ability of the democratic forces, parties, movements, and trade unions to organize themselves to challenge successfully the formal monopoly and in-formal organizational hegemony of the Communist party.

For that the democratic forces in Eastern Europe must be able to organize and offer viable political and economic alternatives. That means talking about alternative policies and not harping on the past crimes of communist regimes. The first is exceedingly difficult to do; the second, unfortunately, comes naturally. Much of the opposition will therefore be decent, noble-minded, and ultimately sterile, since politics is about real-world alternatives. These forces of reform will include both those who are organized or sympathetic to the present alternative groups and the reformist wings of the ruling Communist parties. The mix will differ from country to country, as will the radicalness of the break with the past and the speed with which new governments begin to construct new democratic societies and political cultures. This, given the powerful forces of nationalism and right-wing populism, will be a stormy and conflict-ridden task.

The anticipation of democratic reforms throughout the bloc raises hopes among a wide political public, perhaps *because* such reforms oc-cur under conditions of a general and visible moral and ideological cri-sis in the communist politocratic regimes. Successful reforms may make the cold war a thing of the past. Whatever the ultimate fate of *per-estroika* (the economic reforms), *glasnost* has had an enormous and positive effect in the Soviet Union and Eastern Europe. Those societies are today less oppressive and freer in ways unimaginable only a few years ago.

Politically Eastern Europe essentially consists of the Warsaw Pact countries—East Germany, Poland, Czechoslovakia, Hungary, Romania, and Bulgaria. All are in trouble and none has a generally agreed upon path of development, no matter how long-range or unpleasant, that would solve its economic and social crises. Most proposals for political and economic reforms put forward by the more liberal wing of the Com-munist parties in the region so far have one thing in common, namely, the continued rule or at least domination of these societies by their Communist parties. But it is precisely the continued political monopoly of these parties that is unacceptable to a growing majority of the popu-lation. Thus the reforms from above are sharply self-limiting in range and only encourage demands for more concessions. In some instances there will be demands to dissolve and prohibit the old Communist par-ties.

Recent developments in Hungary and Poland represent attempts in different ways to deal with this dilemma. In Hungary the party has in effect split and the old reform wing is trying to reemerge, new name and all, as a quasi-Social Democratic party. In Poland the party has had to accept Solidarity as a temporarily dominant political competitor. In both cases, however, the party or its majority retains a massive presence in the military, police, civil service, and managerial hierarchies of their societies.

The non-Communists are suffered to play a role within the system, and even a formally leading role in some cases, *on probation*. That is, they are tolerated for the time being, and it is a very open question what the fate of these experiments will be if the grim economic picture does not improve through successful reforms and with massive aid from the West. More ambiguous is the fate of East Germany, which is moving into reforms at a rapid pace forced by implacable pressures from below and constant social and economic hemorrhaging caused by the mass emigration of the young and talented. Unlike the other Eastern European politocracies, the very existence of the German Democratic Republic as a separate state is highly problematic. It would not survive the test of a plebiscite on German unification or its own continued existence. On the other hand, the nation's economic prospects are by far the best in the region. It already has the best-developed economy of all Eastern European countries, and above all it has the Federal Republic of Germany, which will not allow it to collapse economically.

In many ways the prognosis for the success of reform in Czechoslovakia is more favorable than that of other Eastern European reforming regimes. Although dismal, its economy has more resources that support reforms, including substantial natural resources and a large and highly skilled working class with a tradition of trade unions and political democracy. Unlike Poland and Hungary, Czechoslovakia has no strong tradition of right-wing populism and anti-Semitism to attract demagogues and make the rebuilding of a democratic political culture more problematic. There is a strong democratic socialist tradition and both a new Social Democratic party and a Socialist party that are emerging with ever greater autonomy from the imposed coalition with the Communists. There are no unmanageable national disputes like those bedeviling Yugoslavia and the Soviet Union. The opposition has existed in an organized underground form for almost twenty years. The problem, as in East Germany, is to organize genuine trade unions and political parties to take advantage of the opening the reforms provide. It is, in other words, not enough for the party to relinquish its legal monopoly; other organized and democratic political and social forces must emerge. After spontaneous pressure from below one needs to organize political participation through a contending multiparty system. In the

German Democratic Republic and Czechoslovakia, Social Democratic parties and trade unionists will clearly play a major role.

Development of New Genuine Unions in Eastern Europe

The decades-long standoff in Eastern Europe between inefficient regimes and a surly and indifferent working class has rested on a tacit social pact that had developed by the 1960s and which is now increasingly being challenged by forces beyond the control of the regimes. Those forces reflect the growing integration of Eastern Europe into the world market under circumstances that make the technological and productivity gap between Eastern Europe and the rest of the world unacceptable. Poland, Hungary, Romania, and Yugoslavia all owe money to the World Bank as well as to private banks, and all are under pressure to increase their exports to meet their payments. It does not help that all, except perhaps Romania, have far more efficient and advanced economies and economic organization than the Soviet Union. That is after all no basis for comparison, and in any case they do not have the Soviet Union's vast natural resources.

In an attempt to resolve the economic problems of these regimes the Soviets have encouraged the Eastern European states to enter the world market, and *there* the rules of the game have an unfortunately universalist character that measures the Eastern European regimes by very different yardsticks from the ones to which they have been accustomed. New rules in the Eastern bloc trading alliance, SEV, require that even *intrabloc* exchanges take place in dollars. This means, for example, that Eastern European countries will have to pay for oil and natural gas in hard currency. They are now obliged to produce goods of reasonable design, quality, and cost if they are to have a chance to export and earn hard currency.

All this amounts to a formula of a continued stagnation and an ongoing stalemate between class forces. Democratic reforms will not really affect this stalemate, since most reforms proposed by the liberal reformers, even by many of the former democratic leftists, would at least initially increase work discipline and unemployment, and further reduce the already low living standards of the workers. This also enhances a consolidation of class consciousness on the part of the workers on the one hand and self-awareness by the middle class and intellectual strata of their separateness on the other. These are increasingly class societies.

Whatever else takes place in Eastern Europe after the turbulent upheavals of 1989, one thing is clearly in the cards. This region will see the development of *genuine* mass trade unions. Some will rise from the wreckage of the official unions as they become transformed into that which they had never been, namely, organizations defending the specific interests of their members and the working class as a whole. In some cases, as in Poland and parts of Yugoslavia, sections of the old official communist trade union leadership will attempt to turn their organizations into genuine unions.

Other unions will develop as well, new and independent, sometimes even in the form of narrow craft unions. Still other unions will develop among the scientific workers and teachers, as in the case of the independent unions in Hungary. All of these and other forms will emerge in response to the opening up of these societies and to the clear threat to the living standards of the workers. Most of the reforms so far proposed would have the workers bearing the brunt of the cost for getting the economies out of the mess into which the communist politocracy has gotten them. These proposals are *not*, incredibly enough, accompanied by any effective mechanisms for equal sacrifice. On the contrary, *most* proposals include greater rewards for those who can operate within the market and for middle-class professionals. Workers are being told that they are technologically redundant and overprotected. The clear and obvious response will be the formation of unions. It does not help that many of the forces emerging in the newly liberalized Eastern European states are middle-class liberal or populist parties who often only barely hide their contempt for manual laborers and who in any case think that any excessive wage egalitarianism is oppressive per se. This is visible in the uncritical acceptance of the ideological defense of the market as the master instrument of economic reform. I am not questioning here the desirability of introducing market principles in the economy as one of the needed measures to leverage the *nomenklatura* out of economic control. What I *do* question is the present love affair many Eastern European reformers have with the "market" as a synonym for the economic dogmas of Milton Friedman and the social policies of Margaret Thatcher. And of course the Communist parties are held responsible for the horrible economic and cultural conditions in these societies. As Walesa said on February 6, 1989, at the opening of the negotiations for the recognition of Solidarity by the Polish government, "The country is ruined, but it was not some elves that ruined it, but a system of exercising authority, that detaches citizens from their rights and wastes the fruits of their labor" (quoted in the *New York Times*, February 7, 1989).

Then of course one should consider that the Communists have given birth to a very specific, warped, antisocial, semicrooked class of entrepreneurs whose skills at cutting legal corners and finding ways through bureaucratic mazes have been sharply honed. These people are used to quick profits and corruption and are not about to invest, even if they had the means, in the kind of dynamic and innovative private sector the economic reformers hope to encourage. One should also pause and consider just how proposals to privatize sections of the economy will work out in real life. Just who will be permitted to buy what parts of the nationalized sectors of the economy, for what price and under what circumstances?

Given the tendency of these societies to insiderism and the manipulation of informal networks, one can guarantee that massive corruption and favoritism will occur during the scramble to privatize and marketize these societies. There are already signs of this in Hungary, and it will be even more common when privatization involves foreign capital buying into nationalized enterprises. The explanation for this is that more money will be at stake, and Eastern European politocratic elites have a low resistance to financial temptation. After all, foreign capital has been known to engage in bribery in other countries, Milton Friedman and the Chicago School notwithstanding. Corruption will be even more of a concern, however, when the would-be buyers come from the old political elites and the local petty capitalists. That is their forte, after all. The new Eastern European petty capitalists will clearly exacerbate class antagonisms through their very visible consumption of luxuries, avoidance of taxes and regulation, and attempts to corrupt local governments and political parties. That is probably unavoidable, but what is essential under those circumstances is that trade unions and genuine Social Democratic parties form to assure that the marketization of these societies does not develop under the worst possible circumstances, which are antisocial and will threaten democracy. Democracy will be vulnerable if it is accompanied by massive corruption, increased class differences, and greater unemployment. At the very least this will lead to the growth of populism, which has a tradition in this region.

My prognosis is that in much of the Soviet Union and Eastern Europe one will be able to talk about the *Mexicanization* of the society, politics, and economy—that is, a mix of private- and state-owned sectors with hybrid political systems that involve elements of free elections, often modified by corruption and deals among elite groups. The political elite will include the local political barons and operators on the national scene, the new rich, technocrats based in the nationalized sectors of the economy, corrupt trade unionists as well as genuine ones, and a plethora of popular organizations, some more real than others. Freedom to travel and freedom of the press and speech will exist, but will be limited to safe reservations where they do not interfere with the real wielding of power. Again, to continue the metaphor of Mexico, this will occur in the context of a highly charged and ambivalent relationship with the dominant regional colossus, in this instance in the East rather than in the North. All this would represent a step forward in the complicated real world we live in, and terrain for further struggles for genuine democracy.

The Changing Political Dependence of Eastern European States

Eastern Europe is no longer an economic asset to the Soviet Union, nor has it been for over two decades. If anything, today it is a drag on Soviet resources. The uncertain political stability of the Eastern European states is also a problem for the Soviets. Given the real prospects for major cutbacks in armaments and general detente in Europe on the part of both military alliances, the Warsaw Pact itself has become less relevant and above all is worthless. The approaching end of the cold war will lead to increasing support for proposals to abolish the two alliances. More problematic is the set of bilateral military agreements the Soviet Union has with individual countries in Eastern Europe. These agreements will probably be retained for some time, since they are regarded as important for Soviet security.

Increasing Eastern European autonomy is evolving into a general "Finlandization" of the area where Soviet strategic and security interests remain protected as greater political and social differentiation of the Eastern European states takes place. An increasingly popular metaphor among analysts of the Soviet bloc of the process leading to the possible Finlandization of Eastern Europe is the rough historical image of the "Ottomanization" of the empire, that is, the parallel of the century-long decline of the Ottoman Empire in which province after province on the periphery gained de facto independence while maintaining a purely pro forma acceptance of Ottoman overlordship. That was how Egypt, Serbia, Bulgaria, and Romania gradually gained their independence from the Turkish empire in the nineteenth century. The problem with this image is that those states *also fought* their Turkish masters, usually with foreign military and diplomatic support. That makes Ottomanization at best a very clumsy metaphor.

The old stereotype about Soviet-Eastern European relations, reinforced in the West by generations of Eastern European political exiles, is today simply wrong, and has been false for over a decade and a half. The Soviet Union does not exploit the Eastern European states economically. Czechoslovakia, Hungary, and Poland are all economically in miserable shape for a number of complicated reasons. Moreover, the Soviet supply of raw materials has allowed them to maintain a relatively higher standard of living than that in the Soviet Union itself. Soviet subsidies to Poland, for example, have created for the Poles a higher standard of living than that of Soviet citizens. This is seen as adding insult to injury, since the Poles are also freer than Soviet citizens and use that freedom in good part to complain about Soviet-Polish relations. On the other hand, Hungarians who for decades benefited from Soviet oil and natural gas prices now insist that the Soviets pay for the Hungarian trade surplus in dollars. Under trade rules established by SEV, this will become standard in intraregional trade as there is less that can be handled by economic barter agreements in the Eastern bloc.

The Soviet model has in the past tended to emphasize heavy industry as critical for any strategy of development. Most of the Eastern European economies, having followed the Soviet model of development, have become heavily dependent on the Soviet Union for both cheap energy and cheap raw materials. As a consequence, for almost three decades the Soviets have been subsidizing their Eastern European dependencies by selling them energy — oil and natural gas, as well as some raw materials — well below world market prices. By the mid-1970s, they could no longer afford to continue these subsidies and began to renegotiate the trade agreements, moving closer to the world market prices calculated in hard currency. Now, those societies face economic disaster, in good part because they are hooked on cheap energy and raw materials.

Even more harmful is the archaic, authoritarian, and overcentralized economic system itself. Reforms will be very difficult to achieve since of course the Soviet economy faces the same problems. That explains the urgency and seriousness with which Gorbachev is pursuing economic reforms as well as detente with the United States, which is essential to provide the breathing space and economic resources for those reforms to have a chance to succeed. Due to the bottlenecks in their own economy, the drop in the world price of oil, and their own need for large-scale imports of Western technology (which must be paid for in hard currencies), the Soviets are less able to aid their allies than in the past. The increasing technological and economic burden of the arms race launched in the last two years of the Carter administration and continued with such fanfare by the Reagan administration had of course exacerbated the already dismal economic scene for the Soviets and consequently for their allies.

This explains the Soviets' obvious and public reluctance to continue their aid to the Sandinistas in Nicaragua and their continual advice for moderation in that country. It also explains their willingness to liquidate the Afghanistan adventure on terms that involve possibly fatal risks for their allies there. For that matter, the current Soviet advice to their friends throughout the Third World is to come to whatever terms possible with the world market—that is, with the "currently existing" world market, controlled by capitalist powers and norms. This represents an obvious massive ideological retreat in the face of the stubborn reality of the failure of the Third World countries that had adopted features of the Soviet economic or political model. It will be particularly unwelcome in Castro's Cuba.

Links between the Eastern European regimes and the Soviet Union today are still there, but they are above all political and military. Of course, the decades-long *insistence* on Soviet-style centrally planned command economies did politically impose an inefficient system throughout the region. This was particularly harmful to developed economies like those of Czechoslovakia and the German Democratic Republic. In that sense the Soviets are clearly historically to blame, and are held responsible by the Eastern European populations, for the miserable economies and despised political leaderships that have brought about the current general economic and social crisis in the region. That the reality is, as always, a good bit more complex does not help much in practical political terms.

The cost of the status quo for Eastern European communist regimes must be counted in political, moral, social, and economic terms, the most overwhelming cost being in the moral and spiritual areas. One not so incidental cost has been that the term "socialism" has been devastated in much of Eastern Europe. Throughout Eastern Europe, not even the party elite believes in "currently existing socialism" anymore—if it ever did. This increasingly widespread ideological vacuum has brought about broad cynicism and apathy about *organized* politics and often even about *organized* oppositional politics, in particular among the young. Social movements are more congenial and appear "purer." This has also spread across class barriers so that there is a genuine youth subculture, one that is mostly apolitical, hedonistic, and materialist. Certain topics, currently ecology and human rights (as distinct from democracy), serve as a focus for single-issue activities, particularly if the issue is fashionable among the young in the West. Rejection of the *language* of socialism does not, however, necessarily extend to the basic values of socialism, namely, democracy, equality, community, and participation. On the contrary, many aspects of that youth culture are antiauthoritarian and egalitarian, and seem open to other-directed goals and activities, provided, always, that this is not stated in the god-awful jargon of official socialism. This in part explains the attractiveness of alternative peace and ecology groups throughout the area.

Alternatives and Opposition in Eastern Europe

Only a small part of the opposition in Eastern Europe today uses an explicitly socialist vocabulary and theoretical and political framework, East Germany and Yugoslavia being the important exceptions. The democratic opposition in Czechoslovakia is more ambivalent, but then it is more "Western," and faith in socialist politics or the left died among Western intellectuals a while ago. On the other hand, the politics of the massive Czech and Slovak working class are social democratic, and the immense popularity of the former leader of communist reformation in Prague in 1968, Alexander Dubček, should give pause to those who think that democratic socialist politics are dead in Czechoslovakia. Solidarity in Poland does not use socialist terminology, but then it is also the dominant force in the present Polish government and not an opposition as such. Rather it is a mass working-class movement with an inchoate presocialist program mixed in with a great deal else, including simple trade unionism, nationalism, populism, and religion. There are a number of democratic Socialist organizations and parties in Poland as well. There are also several right-wing nationalist organizations, and the popularity of right-wing liberalism (in the European sense of the word, that is, free marketing and antistatist) is increasing.

In practice, much of the struggle of the opposition in Eastern Europe had, quite rightly, centered on the question of democratic rights and liberties. A favorite quotation is one from the Soviet dissident Butkovsky: "We are not from the left camp or the right camp. We come from the concentration camp." Democracy therefore remains the primary demand. This is indeed a good thing despite the ambivalence of a generation of miseducated Marxists in both Western and Eastern Europe about so-called bourgeois democracy.

I personally do not accept the notion that there is such a thing as "bourgeois" democracy or liberty. These are democratic rights and liberties that have been won from the bourgeoisie in over a century and a half of bloody struggles. In any case the struggle for democracy and liberty predates the struggle for socialism. These are democratic rights and liberties that today happen to exist primarily in bourgeois societies. These liberties and democratic rights are safest, however, in those bourgeois societies with the most powerful workers' political parties and movements. For that matter, non-working-class autonomous social movements are strongest and most effective in those societies with powerful working-class Socialist parties and movements and traditions. These are not "bourgeois liberties," and one of the not so minor problems with the contemporary socialist project in much of the world is that some Socialists still think of those liberties as time-bound and relevant only for bourgeois societies.

Even worse is the prattle about democracy and individual rights being a specifically "Western" preoccupation. The struggle for human rights is therefore dismissed as a form of Western cultural imperialism; that is, it is refuted by the immense size and importance of repressive institutions in "non-Western" states and in Third World "socialist" societies.

It seems reasonable, on the part of the working-class movements and activists or for that matter any other popular democratic movements in Eastern Europe and the Soviet Union, to say, "We want at least *all* the liberties workers have in the Western world, and then we want more." What is certain is that they do not want *fewer* rights than workers in Western Europe—they want *more* rights. That would seem a reasonable thing to demand from a government calling itself a socialist government ruling in the name of the working class.

Trade union gains, even the legalization of alternate unions, that did not include a relatively autonomous judiciary and widespread political freedoms clearly would not be worth the paper they were written on. They could be rescinded the next morning. Thus one cannot separate trade union demands, particularly in politocratic regimes, from certain broad democratic political demands. It is doubtful whether the Polish regime would actually have granted even limited trade union rights if Solidarity had not also appeared as a wider social movement with very broad social and political legitimacy.

The legalization of Solidarity in the spring of 1989 occurred in the context of Soviet reforms and a successful foreign policy initiative by Gorbachev. The negotiations also were carried out at a time when economic conditions were far worse than in 1981 and the regime was desperate to get Solidarity to share power and, above all, responsibility for maintaining the economy and for moving on to some rationalizing reforms. That is, the negotiations took place in a framework in which Soviet intervention, against the legalization of Solidarity as an alternate union, and its domination of the first noncommunist government in Eastern Europe are very unlikely indeed. Poland neatly illustrates the difference between "government" (dominated by Solidarity) and "regime" (dominated, still, by the Communist party).

Despite its tactical ambivalence Solidarity has become the protest movement of a very wide sector of society—the peasantry, as well as the intelligentsia; for example, in the Gdansk agreements it raised women's demands that were very advanced. In state "socialist" regimes the demand for democracy is the primary socialist demand. Everything begins with that—with freeing the society from the total domination of the party and the state. This creates the space for autonomous social, cultural, political, and popular institutions and thus for the emergence of a truly civil society.

Reformist struggles for continued reform and transformation of state socialist regimes in the immediate future may well depend more on many autonomous social movements, which are harder to repress, than on explicit and therefore visible and repressible socialist opposition. As has been demonstrated in the past, reformist struggles can be enormously militant, particularly as popular movements gain a sense of confidence and empowerment through limited but real victories. Nevertheless the goal of the democratic opposition has to be the creation of a legal order in which the judiciary system is independent of the state, a richly varied civil society that is autonomous from the state and the dominant political parties, genuine mass democratic trade unions, and a multiparty parliamentary democracy. In other words, the democratic opposition must seek to move beyond the arena of the social movements to *institutionalize* a democratic state and organizations.

These are necessary but not sufficient prerequisites for the struggle for genuine socialist democracy, which would include workers' control in the workplaces, popular grass-roots participatory authority in the various institutions, and the abolition of gender oppression. However, these democratic socialist and feminist goals are not *counterpoised* to the institutionalization of a democratic polity; on the contrary, fighting for these goals *requires* a democratic polity. A parliamentary democracy with powerful unions, parties, and social movements is the optimal terrain on which to work for democratic socialism.

Summary

The Soviet Union and Eastern Europe today face major economic, social, and political crises. The presence of a large and increasingly dissatisfied industrial working class will produce continual pressure from below in these systems, which will encourage both liberalizing and technocratic reform movements from above and openings toward greater democracy.

In response to these crises Soviet leadership under Mikhail Gorbachev is extraordinarily open to radical cutbacks in military expenditures and arsenals and is moving to end the cold war. The end of the cold war opens exciting possibilities for continued democratic change in Eastern Europe. Western Europe and the United States should facilitate both the chances of successful reforms in the Soviet bloc and the end of the present cold war confrontation, which has been the linchpin of the post-World War II social and economic order. Although supportive of the liberalization and economic reforms from above, Western supporters of democracy should also be particularly active in maintaining contact with and nurturing the tender shoots of democracy from below and developments toward genuine civil societies. To do this, extensive contacts, official and unofficial, government and opposition, should be encouraged and expanded between the socialist, peace, and labor movements in the West in general and Western Europe in particular, as well as those in the Soviet alliance.

Soviet leaders should be told amicably but firmly that the degree of contact and friendliness depends on the continued opening up of these societies and expansion of democratic and individual human rights, rather than linking aid, as the Bush administration wants, to the Soviet abandonment of Cuba and Nicaragua to the tender mercies of Washington. This is exactly the kind of superpower deal that should be rejected, since it perpetuates the notion born during the cold war that it is up to the United States and the Soviet Union to decide the fate of small countries and the world. The end of the cold war will necessarily also come to mean the end of a world order dominated by the superpowers. Terminating the cold war is not something that should be done to "reward" the Soviets; rather, it is in the genuine interest of the vast majority of the world. It is therefore also in the interest of the people of the United States.

NOTES

1. A very short and idiosyncratic bibliography on the crisis of the Eastern European and Soviet systems would include: Isaac Deutscher's biography of Trotsky, or at least its first two volumes, *The Prophet Armed* and *The Prophet Disarmed* (New York: Oxford University Press, 1954); Stephen F. Cohen and Robert C. Tucker (eds.), *The Great Purge Trial* (New York: Grosset and Dunlap, 1965); Paul Sweezy, *Post Revolutionary Society* (New York: Monthly Review Press, 1976); Fernando Claudin, *The Communist Movement: From the Comintern to the Cominform*, 2 vols. (New York: Monthly Review Press, 1975). See also George Kennan, *Russia and the West under Lenin and Stalin* (Boston: Little, Brown, 1960); Seweryn

Bialer (ed.), *The Domestic Context of Soviet Foreign Policy* (Boulder: Westview, 1981); Charles Gati and Jan Triska (eds.), *Blue Collar Workers in Eastern Europe* (London: Allen and Unwin, 1981); Walter D. Connor, *Socialism, Politics, and Equality* (New York: Columbia University Press, 1979); Mark Rakovski (pseudonym), *Towards an East European Marxism* (New York: St. Martin's Press, 1978). To these could be added Bogdan Denitch, *Limits and Possibilities: The Crisis of Yugoslav Socialism and State Socialist Systems* (Minneapolis: University of Minnesota Press, 1990).

   2. A lengthy discussion is found in Denitch, *The Socialist Debate: Beyond Red and Green* (London: Pluto Press, 1990), chapters 2 and 3. A shorter discussion can be found in *Limits and Possibilities*.

Chapter 4

European Social Democracy: The Neocorporatist Compromise

Social democracy, all its existing ambiguities and problems notwithstanding, seems destined, through a series of historical developments, to be the dominant organizational and ideological force in Western European politics for the foreseeable future. This in turn positions European social democracy to play a decisive role in developments in *Eastern* Europe and the Soviet Union. This is because it is the existing model of welfare state capitalism in Western Europe that has been shaped in large part by social democracy, rather than some abstract neoliberal model of pure market-driven capitalism, and which will most directly influence the development of Eastern European and Soviet economic and social reforms. In other words, the model of capitalism most accessible to the Eastern European reforms will be welfare state capitalism. After all, it is the specific form of capitalism in the western European nations that will be most involved in trade and technological and other exchanges with the reforming politocratic regimes in the East.

One reason this opening for social democracy exists in Eastern Europe today is that "Anglo-Saxons' " ideologically motivated, class confrontational politics would be a clear disaster, even if they were desirable or even remotely possible, in the state "socialist" regimes moving toward democratic and economic reforms. Any attempt to apply "Thatcherism," that is, to launch an assault on the minimal safety nets provided by the crude universal welfare states in Eastern Europe, combined with union bashing directed against the new genuine unions in those states, would create social strains and class antagonisms that would jeopardize democratic reforms. The strains would make it all but impos-

64

sible for the new postcommunist governments to achieve any democratic legitimacy.

Social democratic policies will be dominant in the new unified Europe as a result of the growing inability of the United State and its British ally to project themselves convincingly as the political leaders or desirable models of political democracies. They are certainly not leaders in the European Economic Community. Moreover, they are patently out of step, both ideologically and politically, with the major thrust of Western European thinking about the future and direction of European unification. One could even convincingly argue that their political systems, both of which are derived from eighteenth-century elite Whig politics, rather than from democratic theories evolved on the European continent since the French Revolution, are out of date. They are certainly out of date when combined with a primitive version of capitalism, which is inconsistent with the needs of a truly modern economy and society.

The brief flirtation with Americophilia and Reaganomics in France and Western Europe during the early years of the Reagan administration seems today to have been more rooted in the brand of perverse theorizing of trendy European intellectuals who have celebrated Jerry Lewis as a great misunderstood acting genius and the Hollywood Western as a pathbreaking cultural achievement of contemporary Western civilization than stemming from any serious attempt to adopt as their own models the economic and social policies that fascinated the Americans and British. In short, the Reaganomics and the United States in question were more products of the fertile imaginations of the New Philosophers and their cothinkers than an effort to understand just how those transatlantic phenomena worked in real life. That particular intellectual fashion is past and nothing similar has as yet replaced it for which we should be thankful. The reality is that U.S. political influence is at a low point in Western Europe today, probably the lowest point since the end of World War II. That fact also necessarily affects the position of the United States' political allies on the Continent with regard to social and economic policies.

Social Democrats Face New Political Opportunities

The fact that politics abhors a power vacuum works to the advantage of the only major contender for legitimate political power in the advanced industrial democracies outside of the United States and its conservative allies — Western European social democracy and the broad so-called Euroleft. This is ironic since this new role of social democracy (i.e., the role of being the obviously dominant integrating force in the European Community) has not been accompanied by any great surge in mass mobilization or enthusiasm for the Social Democratic parties and movements. Rather, they are more generally viewed as the lesser evil, the obvious, if not terribly exciting, alternative.

My own attitude toward European social democracy has been mixed. It clearly *is* the lesser evil, or rather the much preferred alternative throughout the advanced industrial democracies of Western Europe. But I wish social democracy would more quietly absorb the lessons from the new social movements and the Greens and provide a more hospitable environment for working out a strategy for moving beyond the advanced welfare state to a democratic socialist society. It is a problem with what President Bush calls the "vision thing." Mass democratic movements need a vision and a long-range program. They also need to struggle, nationally and internationally, against injustice and inequality with greater militancy. In the meantime the Social Democrats are the best game in town, and so I guess I should accept the label of left-wing Social Democrat. Part of my discomfort lies in knowing that *the realization of any* social democratic program, left, right, or center, in my own country (the United States) would be a giant step forward. It is therefore problematic, sterile, and somewhat abstract for democratic socialists in the U.S. to be overcritical of their European counterparts.

This familiarity with social democracy means that it is less traumatic for the middle classes and the capitalist class to accept, albeit reluctantly, social democratic electoral victories or governments as perhaps unpleasant but legitimate. That same familiarity, unfortunately for the Social Democratic parties, also fails to inspire mass mobilization from below. It also makes it increasingly difficult to keep recruiting and retaining young members and activists. Social democratic governments do not promise to transform their societies, to make the lives of the mass of the people fundamentally different, at least not in the immediate future. Instead, they propose to improve, steadily and continuously, the conditions of the less prosperous two-thirds of the population within the familiar and slow framework of parliamentary democracy.

European Social Democrats do not promise the same chiliastic individual and collective fulfillment and engagement revolutionary movements do. Instead, they offer a politics of the possible. While such a concept inspires confidence in broad segments of the electorate, it does not generate commitment among movement activists and intellectuals. As a consequence, the significance of the increasing social democratic domination of Europe is all too often overlooked and consistently underestimated. Sometimes social democratic politics are dismissed as being merely "Eurocentric." This is particularly the case when it comes to intellectuals and other trendsetters in Western Europe and the United States. Whatever else one can say about social democracy, it is not culturally exciting; it does not give the certainty of being on the side of the elect revolutionary cadre threatening bourgeois society itself, as various forms of Maoism and other far-left sectarianism did. It does not generate new fashions like pseudoguerrilla costumes sported by sympathizers with Third World revolutionaries and the Red Brigade. Posters of contemporary European leaders will never grace student dorms—none of them looks anywhere nearly as funky as Che Guevara, Angela Davis, or Chairman Mao. Of course the posters of apologists for or practitioners of murderous totalitarian politics were the symbols of a sensibility that is all but dead. No movements can live off such a tradition, since it is impossible to feed off dead matter. In any case, leaders of mass democratic movements and parties should not be celebrated with iconographic posters, which were often just a way of saying no to the existing social order rather than a positive statement. What the Social Democrats offer is an affirmative political program, but one that, in the words of Irving Howe, calls for steady work rather than dramatic breakthrough.

A genuine broad and democratic left, one that can improve the lives of millions in advanced industrial societies and in the Third World, needs something beyond a politics of protest and negation; it needs a positive program, one that can stand the test of the hurly-burly of democratic political contestation and win honest majorities. Even a modest reformist program, if that is all that is possible, would suffice. Nevertheless contemporary social democracy is changing the rules of the game politically in a fundamental way and is reshaping political culture and the social parameters of life in the advanced industrial European democracies. If these efforts succeed, the European Community will be in a position to address the problem of the desperately poor South.

Today programmatic disorientation appears to exist within most, if not all, of the mass Socialist and Social Democratic parties of the advanced industrial world, at least on the theoretical and ideological level; this is not reflected electorally, however. This particular ideological semicrisis seems to have been temporarily solved or at least postponed to a distant and undetermined future by a shift in the definition of the strategy and goals of European social democracy. That shift has two effects. First, it makes organized social democracy openly a defender of broad-based progressive social policies and the welfare state rather than a movement committed to a fundamental transformation of the social order to some kind of an as yet undefined socialism. Second, in departing from the traditional postwar Keynesian program, which focused almost exclusively on economic demands, Social Democratic parties have become much more sensitive to new emerging political publics on the broad left; that is, they have become more sensitive to feminism and ecology. In this respect the parties of the right and center cannot really begin to compete with them, for they are far too out of sympathy with the women's movements and with environmental activists. Socialist parties, on the other hand, have been busily co-opting parts of the demands and programs of those movements throughout Europe.

This programmatic shift broadens the basis of support of social democracy beyond its traditional trade union and productivistic clientele to include increasingly both the clients of the welfare state and the social movements. It also protects it somewhat from the inevitable, if unjust, backwash of having to accept some of the blame for the grotesque caricatures of socialism that are collapsing throughout the old Soviet bloc. It is protected from being associated with those regimes in the mind of the political publics through avoiding any rash promises to establish something called socialism. *That* has been postponed in practice to the distant future, and the shape of that "socialism" is sufficiently vague as to appear unthreatening.

Although this solves the organizational and electoral problem of the broad Western European left and strategically positions it politically to dominate the unified European Community, it leaves unsolved the more general crisis in morale created by the absence of a clearly agreed on socialist "project." One could also be somewhat cynical about a socialism that frightens no one, not even the rich and greedy. In other words, while the wealthy, except in few cases, fairly consistently vote against the Social Democrats, they do not seem to think their very existence as a class is in question. Rather, the worst they face with social democratic governments is more progressive taxation, some power sharing in the economy with unions and the state, and a generally more egalitarian social climate created by the widespread and generous social programs of an advanced welfare state. All these are indeed desirable, especially from the vantage point of a United States whose social and economic policies are ever more backward, but they are hardly the stuff of which barricades, or right-wing armed coups such as the one that overthrew Allende in Chile, are made. In short, these programs and reforms do not require that political legitimacy be challenged head-on, and therefore social democratic governments, at least in Europe, cannot be toppled by direct extraparliamentary pressures and assaults on the legal order. They *can* govern, and do so effectively.

In response to the assertion that there is a crisis of socialism or a crisis of morale among socialist movements in advanced industrial societies, one can claim with some firmness that ideological disorientation is hardly limited to contemporary socialism. To be exact, contemporary liberalism is not exactly basking in self-confidence; authoritarian communism is in an irreversible crisis; and the moral and political credentials of American "raw" capitalism are in tatters around the world, as confirmed by the masses of homeless people on the streets of American cities and the mounting toll of the victims of the United States Third World clients.

After all, it is this rejection of established overarching worldviews and models that is characteristic of our decade! It has bred whole new schools of academic criticism like deconstructionism and postmodernism that have spread through the universities of Western Europe and the United States. From that vantage point in the academy these theories are spreading into the media in the usual vulgarized way that complex ideas get simplified and consumed. Thus socialism, at least democratic socialism, is in no worse an intellectual crisis than other systemic worldviews. Organizationally and electorally, the Socialist parties are clearly not in crisis; on the contrary, they are on the rise.

While this is all true, it provides no response to the critics of the Social Democrats *within* their own political publics. A crisis of confidence of a movement theoretically committed to a fundamental change in the social order, in the status quo, is obviously a more serious problem than similar crises for supporters of the existing social, economic, and political order. The most elementary of the claims of the classic conservative defenders of the status quo is that basic social, political, or economic change is itself dangerous, undesirable, or quite simply impossible.

The most basic of the claims by the left historically in general, and therefore also of the Socialists, has been that democratic politics are possible; that it is possible for ordinary men and women to make effective changes in their societies, to do so in their own interest, and to make those changes democratically; that it is possible for those traditionally excluded from power, the so-called objects of history, to become its subjects, for the passive objects of politics and the economy consciously to take charge of their societies. This essentially democratic rather than liberal belief, and not the belief in state or social ownership of industry or confidence in centrally planned economies or the achievement of high economic growth rates, is fundamental to democratic socialism today. That is one of the historical lessons derived from the years of experimentation by the Communists.

Neocorporatist Compromise: What Balance of Forces?

The Continental social democratic and trade union leaderships have to deal with a less confrontational business community than their British and American counterparts. Also present on the political scene in Europe is a social Catholicism that has been as ambivalent about "raw," classically liberal capitalism as it has been about socialism. This has created political space for a wide consensus around an extended welfare state, an interventionist state as far as the economy was concerned, and a general commitment to a welfare state economy that has attenuated class conflict. During the first postwar decades extensive social welfare states had therefore become the norm throughout Western and Northern Europe. The tasks of reconstruction and the takeoff afforded by the Marshall Plan provided both unprecedented full employment and steady and high growth. Considerable corporatist welfare state legislation had already been placed on the books by the Nazis in Germany, Mussolini in Italy, and the Pétain government in Vichy France. This corporatist legislative heritage, which included among other things prenatal child allowances, remained intact after the war. For that matter, widespread nationalization in France and Italy also was the direct result of the war; some enterprises were already state-owned, and others were nationalized to punish the owners for collaborating with the Fascists. Whatever the roots, this corporatist heritage blended easily into the postwar neocorporatist compromise, since it was accepted by both the social Catholics and the Socialists. Thus the nationalization of sectors of the economy did not necessarily have its origins in left-wing legislation, just as the first extensive social legislation in Europe, let us remember, was produced by Bismarck in order to weaken the political attraction of the socialist left. Be that as it may, this *also* provides a far wider base of legitimacy for such measures, since their support is not limited to the left.

During the postwar years of Keynesian orthodoxy and prolonged growth it was widely believed, by both left and right, that capitalist cycles and depressions were a thing of the past. A steadily rising living standard for the working class, achieved without excessive efforts on the part of their parties and unions, dramatically transformed the social landscape of Western Europe. The traditional parties of the right, which could have been expected to oppose progressive social legislation and the growing influence of the unions, had been for the most part discredited through their collaboration with the Nazis or their lack of support for the Resistance. The left in general had played a dominant role in the

Resistance. While the military value of the antifascist and anti-Nazi Resistance was often mythified and exaggerated past all common sense, its symbolic value in salving the wounded national pride and soothing the queasy consciences of the occupied Western European countries was great. The right could not assail the socialist left as being unpatriotic and antinational; on the contrary, the antifascist imagery of World War II was more consistent with the politics of the left. This weakened the right in Europe for the first postwar decade, during which Western European welfare state policies were shaped.

A new, essentially nonconflictual social compact between the major class contenders seemed to have been reached through the creation of huge internal "Fordist" markets throughout Western Europe, thereby increasing the incomes and thus the purchasing power of the working classes. This social compact endured for at least two solid decades after the war. And it was not a sellout by the Socialists and trade unions; rather it was a two-way deal. I believe a better and tougher deal could have been made, but then that is a sterile historical dispute today. It is the old "what if . . ." question.

The cold war led to substantial economic and political concessions to the socialist and Catholic trade unions to help them replace the communist unions. This seemed to make sense from a standpoint of "security" in the late 1940s and early 1950s when genuine fears existed that the cold war might become hot. This led in turn to compromises between the Socialists, who were junior allies of the United States in part because of the Labour government in Britain, and European industrialists. After all, Willy Brandt was the socialist mayor of the West Berlin that defied the Communist blockade in the early 1950s with the U.S. airlift of vital supplies. It was not always a one-way alliance, however. There was also the time when the United States sent military supplies and wheat to help Tito's Yugoslavia to maintain its independence. In any case, Keynesian-regulated, stable postwar economic growth assured that national economies were no longer perceived as zero-sum games in which the gain of one group could only be at the expense of another. On the contrary, the economy and society were a growing pie with plenty of slices for all.

Western European welfare state policies were developed during the economically optimistic and politically consensual postwar years and since then have become established rights to be defended by their beneficiaries. The creation of an extensive welfare state automatically expanded the clientele of the Socialist and labor-oriented parties throughout Europe. It also created masses of white-collar workers and professionals in the welfare state bureaucracies who were prone to unionization and tended to vote left, and therefore the era of the "end of ideology" never resulted in the often predicted lowering of the left vote. Nor did a decrease in the percentage of blue-collar voters mean a smaller vote for the Socialists. Quite the contrary.

Less clear than the stability and growth of the left vote was what that vote meant politically. What do those who vote for the socialists want? However, the welfare state was, and remains, immensely popular, even if the nationalization of industry is not. Planning is a more ambiguous question, since a great deal of state intervention and planning takes place in Western European economies whether the Socialists are in office or not. It is therefore a nonissue. Social entitlement programs and almost twenty-five years of prosperity and growth, unprecedented in the history of modern capitalism, have resulted in steadily improving living standards, which have revolutionized the conditions of the working class throughout Western Europe.

Immediately after the war, armed with a large majority and a moral hegemony based on collective sacrifices that had been necessary to win the war, the Labour party in Britain had a major chance to set the pattern for socialist policies for all Europe. Britain was one of the victors, Europe was war-torn. In dealing with the economy, British Socialists made the first of the classic mistakes of postwar social democracy by inventing "lemon socialism." They nationalized industries that were losing money and that had been terribly undercapitalized over the years — railways, coal mines, shipyards. The result was that these industries, essential to the general infrastructure of the British economy, had to be run at a loss, and subsidized by tax revenues, thus "proving" the economic inefficiency of nationalization as well as Socialists in government in general.

To make things worse the British public enterprise provided an administrative structure in nationalized industries that was as authoritarian as the one in private industry had been. There was certainly every reason not to begin a program of nationalization with sectors of the economy that had been milked to exhaustion by the previous owners and would require permanent state subsidies. This was done to avoid excessive confrontation with the old ruling class, but the effect was to allow that class to maintain itself and to bail it out by buying out money-losing industries like railroads and coal mines. In any case the British Labour party was deeply suspicious of any variety of workers' control from below. Both of its dominant traditions encouraged bureaucratic nationalization. The Fabians were explicitly elitist whereas the trade union bureaucrats would no more permit democracy in industry than they would in their own unions.

By the late 1960s the Labour party began to enter its long-drawn-out programmatic crisis. Within a decade the party appeared to have created a permanent Conservative majority. At stake was and is the very identity of the Labour party and socialism in Britain. That identity will be resolved only when the Labour party becomes more like European Social Democratic parties. Accomplishing this will require giving up certain hallowed political myths dear to intransigent "leftists," but perhaps more to the point it will mean giving up the two most visible albatrosses around the neck of the British Labour party. The first is the trade union block vote, which is clearly undemocratic, and the equally undemocratic and very English commitment to the first-past-the-post electoral system. The latter treats elections as a sort of lottery rather than as a process through which the democratic will of the electorate shapes the government. The Labour party keeps hoping to win at the lottery, which would give it the same unfair advantage that has permitted Thatcher to govern with a minority of votes.

At Bad Godesberg in 1959 the German Social Democrats voted out the remaining vestiges of a claim to be a party based on class struggle and described themselves as a "people's" party working for an advanced and egalitarian welfare state in a mixed, essentially capitalist economy firmly committed to Keynesianism.[1] By the 1960s the German SPD became more self-confident and assertive and put itself forward with some conviction as the alternate governing party of West Germany. To achieve this it first had to painfully reconstruct the most powerful and massive labor movement in Europe. The Swedish labor movement has organized a much larger proportion of the work force, but the difference in size of the two countries is enormous. West Germany is the industrial giant and the natural economic leader of the European Community. This is why the West German social democratic movement is dominant in the Socialist International and is the pacesetter in Europe.

To achieve the status of the alternate legitimate governing party the German Social Democrats had to go through a long process of adaptation, in the face of hostility from a United States that wielded a great deal of influence in Germany at the time. This adaptation included years in coalition with the Christian Democrats in the "Grand Coalition" of the 1960s and then government under both Willy Brandt and Helmut Schmidt during which the SPD proved that it could govern competently and do so in the interests of a political public that extended far beyond industrial workers. The Social Democrats took widely supported foreign policy initiatives in Eastern Europe and the Third World that set West Germany and the Social Democrats on a long-range collision course with U.S. foreign policy and with the Americans' dominant role in the Western European alliance.[2] This makes the SPD a major player in the future of a unified EEC after 1992.

The Growing Social Democratic Dominance in Europe

This is not the first time socialism has been in an ideological and intellectual crisis. The fact that the crisis of socialism is a recurrent phenomenon permits some mild optimism about the outcome of the current one. For example, although a fair to middling student of the history of socialist movements, I cannot remember *one* period of the history of contemporary socialism when it was *not* in crisis. The idea was in such disarray in the early part of the nineteenth century that Karl Marx and Friedrich Engels called their manifesto the *Communist* Manifesto to distinguish it from other confused and utopian varieties of socialism. They felt that for purposes of clarification Engels needed to write another pamphlet, this one called "Socialism, Scientific and Utopian." And a fine polemic against all sorts of confused fellow Socialists it was. This did not seem to do much good, since no sooner did the unification of the various socialist currents in Germany produce the first mass Social Democratic party than Marx felt it essential to write his positively vitriolic "Critique of the Gotha Program." The bulk of the written tradition of the socialist movement consists of such polemics against programs and views that are supposedly leading the movement into fatal crisis.

It was at the end of a decade of such continual crises that the labor-based Social Democratic parties achieved their widest electoral gains only to be temporarily turned back by the prolonged economic crisis that followed the oil shock of 1973. It is during the present crisis of the late 1980s that the Socialists, with their Italian Communist allies, have come to constitute the plurality in the European Parliament. If one adds the Greens, who mostly vote with the Socialists and the other fragments of the left, that plurality is quite large and growing. Indications are that both the Federal Republic and Great Britain will soon have socialist, or Socialist-dominated, governments.

The labor-based parties have not yet fully caught up with the tactical consequences and strategic possibilities of their present and growing plurality in the European Parliament and the increased importance of the EEC. Local elections in both France and Sweden in 1988 went very well indeed for the Socialists. Opinion polls throughout 1989 even showed major gains by Labour in Thatcherite Great Britain, a trend confirmed by the smashing victory of the Labour party in the European parliamentary elections in the spring of 1989.

Since virtue is sometimes rewarded in politics the SPD should be able to reap benefits from the most obvious, albeit indirect, product of its *Ostpolitik*, namely, the fact that German unification now appears possible in the very near future. This will not only retrospectively have proved the wisdom of Brandt's initiatives in Eastern Europe and confidence-building measures in the Soviet Union, but will have a more direct benefit of producing masses of new Social Democratic voters in any German federation that includes the GDR and its electorate.

Even in Mediterranean Europe the Socialist parties are doing well organizationally and electorally. To be sure, exaggerated hopes that they would be *more* radical than the far stronger and better organized Northern European parties were always illusory. It is simply that so long as they had no prospects of being in power there was no limit to how radical their oratory and slogans could be. As they grew stronger it became clear that they had valid and important tasks to perform in democratizing and modernizing their societies and helping to integrate them into Europe. What they could not do is build advanced welfare states, let alone attempt to build socialism. They cannot have been expected to be that, given the much weaker organizations and trade unions in their societies. All talk of a radical anticapitalist French socialist program was less relevant than the small percentage of unionized workers and the weak party organization. The same is even more the case in Greece or Portugal, or with the Italian Socialists where the *real* party of social democracy is the Italian Communist party, which has finally acknowledged this fact and now makes possible a serious left majority in that country. In Spain the Socialists are hegemonic as the democratic and modernizing party; in time they will be pushed further to the left by pressures from inside *and* outside their party. Greece is a clear example of a pseudoradical Socialist party. The Greek party PASOK and its leader, Papandreou, have been the darlings of Western European and American leftists, not to mention the Greek electorate, because of a nationalist, populist, anti-American, and Third Worldist demagoguery that was used as a substitute for an effective and egalitarian domestic program. Nevertheless all these parties add to the strength of the socialist bloc in the European Parliament and increase pressure for a social Europe, since that would help most in the least developed areas with the weakest social programs. Those would be leveled upward.

The Socialist parties of Western Europe therefore appear to be recovering from the electoral and organizational doldrums of the early 1980s. Their steady revival, backed up by recent electoral trends and trade union strength throughout Western Europe, is paralleled by greater confidence in a Europe independent of the superpowers. François Mitterrand's electoral victory in France and the Socialists' increased strength in Belgium and Norway, as well as within the European Community, should give pause to those who hastened to see the present crisis of socialism as a final one. A crisis is after all both a challenge and an opportunity. What one can make out of such opportunities will depend a great deal on the fate of the continued success of existing models of social democratic governments. The most obvious such case is Sweden, which therefore remains of interest to all who would speculate about the direction in which social democratic policies will probably move in Europe.

Sweden is not that much ahead programmatically of the most important and powerful Social Democratic party in Europe, the German SPD. Both have played and are continuing to play a very active role internationally in helping weaker Socialist parties in Southern Europe and in the Third World. The Swedish party, however, has had many more years of experience in power and has had to deal with the problem of administering an advanced welfare state through thick and thin, in good times and bad, for generations. It has been in power for so long it has reshaped Swedish society.

Sweden, a Social Democratic Model

Sweden has a highly developed and widely popular welfare state, a mass Socialist party, and the vast majority of the working population—blue collar, white collar, and pink collar, old working class and new working class—is organized in trade unions. To be exact, over 85 percent of Swedish workers are unionized, a figure that tops 90 percent for blue-collar manual workers. This is out of all proportion to the percentage of workers organized in other industrial democracies. Indeed, it is so great a degree of organization that it inevitably affects the political culture itself.

Social Democratic parties with a high degree of organization and a massive membership produce a thick network of allied organizations, women, youth, and cultural. These in turn help create a movement subculture, not unlike that of Italian communism or the classical social democracy in Germany or Austria preceding World War I. This essentially egalitarian and empowering political culture makes these groups more resistant to the influence of Americanization or the mass consumerist culture of the social and cultural scene.

But there is another advantage that "thick" social democratic movements have. A labor movement as massive as the Swedish one is automatically much less narrow and parochially trade unionist in its demands because it has a far larger percentage of workers and thus represents a genuine cross section of the population that is organized. Since it speaks for a broad spectrum of the population it uses the language of universal entitlement rather than narrow economic interests of groups of workers.

Swedish unions have concentrated on defending full, well-paid, and secure employment for all, rather than specific jobs. The result is that unions in Sweden have not been an obstacle to the modernization of their economy and the fundamental shift from traditional smokestack industries to the more modern mix of high technology and services. This factor has given the Swedish labor movement a greater legitimacy and political leverage than exists in any other advanced industrial country and has produced neither high unemployment nor high inflation, nor for that matter technological backwardness. As a result, the number of hours worked per week and during a working life has steadily declined. This increase in leisure time has led to an ongoing emphasis on adult engagement and education, which in turn continually expands the number of people involved in the vast network of organizations, study circles, people's parks, and all of the other popular institutions that help make the Swedish social democratic movement politically and morally hegemonic in that society. Swedish Socialists come by their majorities honestly in a democratic system practicing proportional representation, a fact that forces them to depend on the votes of either the small Eurocommunist party of the left or the ecologists to maintain a parliamentary majority. The effect is that it has far greater political legitimacy as the natural party of government.

A ruling Swedish Social Democratic party actually proposed to move irretrievably beyond the boundaries of capitalism and the welfare state to social ownership in a plan for the collective transfer of stocks to bodies elected by unions, employees, and the local community. The proposal known as the Meidner Plan was defeated after a frantic campaign against it by the bourgeois parties and is now on the back burner. In the meantime, and most of us spend most of our lives "in the meantime," Swedish Socialists defend the welfare state with its concomitant of full employment and social and economic egalitarianism at a time when those modest but essential victories of the workers' movement have been under general attack in so many of the advanced industrial societies of the West. This is in a period when many of the other Labor and Socialist parties have been willing to accept, no matter how reluctantly, the necessity of at least some cutbacks in social spending. Sweden is almost the only nation today in which one hears elected mainline politicians explain that unemployment is not inevitable, or god-given, but the product of human policies, and that therefore full employment, or the closest equivalent to it even under welfare capitalism, is also the product of human agency. Austria has similar low unemployment rates, and the Austrian Socialists also reject the proposition that social policy cannot control unemployment. These two small economies remain a challenge to those who argue that the range of options in employment policies is limited and that unemployment is unavoidable.

The Swedish labor movement has been able to veto hostile legislation through extraparliamentary pressure, which is normally wielded by capital, both nationally and internationally, in most of the rest of the world. This is so much taken for granted that it is used as an argument against egalitarian social policies or progressive taxation; that is, capital would block such measures by a strike of money, in other words by transferring funds elsewhere. During the brief period of "bourgeois" parliamentary majority in the early 1980s the trade unions had effectively blocked any cutbacks in the welfare state and social spending measures. What the Swedish labor movement argued, in a way that might profoundly shock some proceduralist liberals, was that the welfare state is every bit as much, and as unnegotiable, a part of the social compact as parliamentary rules of the game themselves. That is, like parliamentary democracy itself, the welfare state is not subject to political bargaining. That again is a democratic rather than a liberal argument about the nature of democratic politics.

Socialist International Networks and Links

An element that will maximize ideological cross-fertilization among the Social Democratic parties is their extensive network of organized international links. On a practical level this network will bring about a gradual forging of joint strategies for dealing with transnational corporations in both the EEC and EFTA, which are being formally merged into a common European economic "space." Transnational organization of capital and business clearly requires transnational strategies by labor and its parties. There will be a struggle to develop a minimal code of conduct for transnational corporations that cannot be successfully imposed in a single country.

The Socialist parties have a number of international coordinating bodies—the Socialist International, the European Socialist Parliamentary Group, the International Federation of Socialist Women, and the International Union of Socialist Youth, through which many of the current leaders of the parties first met. Paralleling these are the International Secretariats of the Unions in the ICFTU, mostly Socialist-dominated, which are assuming more importance.

While these international institutions of the labor and socialist movement are sometimes weak and primarily symbolic, symbols are important. In any case they form a stable network linking the social democratic institutions internationally in a way that has no parallel for the bourgeois parties. The closest equivalent would be the Catholic parties and unions. Of course *international* organizations of Catholic unions will find a great deal in common with the Socialist-led unions when it comes to dealing with transnationals. The Socialist-dominated trade union international, the ICFTU, is also absorbing reformed unions from Eastern Europe.

Left outside this network of international cooperation (which is essential if labor is to have any chance of dealing with the new international economic environment) are the two cold-war-bred dinosaurs. One is the old Communist-run World Federation of Democratic Trade Unions, which is visibly dissolving. The other is the international operation of the AFL-CIO, which has been compromised beyond redemption by the long years spent in the trenches of the cold war with unsavory right-wing clients of the CIA and the United States in general. It is to be hoped that the end of the cold war can lead to some rethinking and restructuring even in the AFL-CIO. After all, if democratic elections and real unions are possible in Eastern Europe, there may even be hope for the AFL-CIO. The day may come when the AFL-CIO leadership will begin systematically to contrast their situation and the conditions of workers who pay dues to them in the United States with the role of labor in Western Europe. Such an examination may lead them to acknowledge that perhaps the United States in general and the wounded American labor movement in particular may learn something from Western Europe and from the Social Democratic parties and trade unions. The problem with American labor has not been that it was Eurocentric; rather it has been invincibly ignorant in its conviction that an Americentric worldview placed it in the center of the world.

NOTES

1.   Several works provide a useful background: Ralf Dahrendorf, *Society and Democracy in Germany* (London: Weidenfeld & Nicolson, 1960); John Carr, *Helmut Schmidt: Helmsman of Germany* (London: Weidenfeld & Nicolson, 1985); William Graf, *The German Left*

since 1945: Socialism and Social Democracy in the German Federal Republic (New York: Cambridge University Press, 1976). To be sure, all general works on European socialism have major sections on West Germany and the SPD.

2. See, for example, Richard Tilford (ed.), *The Ostpolitik and Political Change in Germany* (London: Saxon House, 1975).

Chapter 5

The Euroleft, Socialists, and the New Social Movements

The Importance of the New Social Movements

Among the unavoidable themes in any contemporary discussion of the state of politics, particularly in the advanced industrial societies of Western Europe, is the relationship of the class-based, more traditional labor and socialist movements, to the new social movements.[1] The importance of this goes beyond the narrow question of the electoral and organizational power of the left; the social movements have become an important cultural phenomenon in industrial societies in general, particularly in industrial democracies. Social movements are one of the ways the important and often informal political mobilization of opinion and activity takes place within civil society. Given the general tendency for the formal political parties to mobilize less energy and enthusiasm from a smaller proportion of the electorate, social movements become increasingly significant. They are, however, most effective in interaction with organized political parties once they have placed an issue on the political or social agenda. This can be seen fairly clearly with regard to issues raised by the women's movements, ecological activists, and the peace movement. Equally important, although not necessarily from the left end of the spectrum, were the issues raised by ethnic, nationalist, anti-immigrant, racist, and some antiracist movements.

As Eastern Europe democratizes further these issues will increasingly become a problem there as well. This can already be seen in the most liberal Yugoslav republic, Slovenia, in the relations between Solidarity and the social movements and parties in Poland, and in Hungary,

81

and will be a growing concern in East Germany and Czechoslovakia as those societies continue to open up. It is a typical problem in societies in which alternative ways of engaging in political activity are open to citizens. Under those circumstances tense, often ambivalent, relations develop between social movements and the political parties that the activists of these movements find more congenial. Activists are frustrated because the parties they prefer do not necessarily place the same priorities on the issues the activists focus on, and in fact the parties resent being pressed to prioritize competing single issues rather than being permitted to focus on general programs. That relationship is rarely analyzed since advocates of the new social movements tend to overstate their case and insist that the new social movements have replaced the more traditional parties of the left (or of the right) as the centers of analysis and activity. On the other hand the supporters of the labor-based mass Social Democratic parties tend to write off the social movements and treat them as essentially a marginal generational phenomenon limited to the university-educated publics. Both, in my opinion, are wrong.

However one conceives of the relationship between the two, these movements are of great importance, particularly in Europe and to the better-educated and younger publics on the left. The first challenge to the "old" Left of the mass working class parties and unions in recent times centered on the issue of the role and significance and eventual class location of the *student movements* of the 1960s. The phenomenon was worldwide, but it can be said to have had three major centers—the United States, France, and West Germany.[2] Those better-educated groups represent expanding segments of the population, the work force and voters who tend to support the left, broadly defined in the West. They also form a disproportionately large part of activists of the alternate and oppositional movements in Eastern Europe. Parties usually seek broad support through coalitions and compromises; movement activists often act as witnesses for their beliefs and issues in their purest form and therefore reject compromise on principle.

Yet parties and social movements both need each other and resent that need. Each seems to feel that its essential character is jeopardized or at least compromised by the other. This is by no means limited to Europe, Eastern and Western. In the United States the relationship between the Republican party and fundamentalists and right-to-life activists is as tense as the relationship between the Democratic party and feminists, gay rights activists, homeless advocates, and anti-interventionism activists. In both cases the "movement" end of the relationship also shows tendencies to organize to replace "party insiders" in taking over the party, as the victory of conservatives in the Republican party and the near victory of Jackson's Rainbow Coalition in the Democratic party demonstrated. The contrast between the United States and Western Europe in this respect rests on the much better organized nature of European political parties. The system itself is more political and responsible in Europe, which is made all but impossible by the organization of party politics in the United States. European parties and most particularly parties of the left are *membership* parties, not mere loose election coalitions. The left political parties have created an alternate political subculture that has no equivalent in the United States.

Trouble with Definitions: What Are Social Movements?

A nagging problem is one of definition. What do we mean by "the left" in Europe, or even only more specifically the left in Western Europe? To what extent is "the left" practically synonymous with the Socialist, Social Democratic, and Labor parties? How significant are the Communist parties for the "Euroleft" today? What, if any, is the role of left-wing Catholics? What should be included under the label of new *social* movements? There is, for example, far wider agreement that new social movements are important than there is about what exactly these movements are.

First the question of the Communist parties. More than half of all organized Communists in Western Europe belong to one party, the Communist party of Italy (PCI). It is by far the largest and most significant Communist party in Europe and is therefore enormously significant for the future of organized communism in advanced industrial capitalist democracies. That the Central Committee of the PCI has decided by an overwhelming and long-expected vote, in the autumn of 1989, to propose that the party change its name, get rid of the party symbol, and apply for full membership in the Socialist International is thus of great, perhaps fatal, importance. This is the end of the long evolution of the party and has removed from the scene, as a distinct and separate *Communist* party, the only one in Western Europe that was dominant on the left in its own country and could conceivably at some point in the future have formed a democratically legitimate government. The PCI is now openly a part of the mainstream social democratic left in Europe. All that awaits is the formalization of this change.

The remaining Communist parties are either more or less significant ginger groups—trying to "ginger" (i.e., liven up) the dominant Social Democratic party in their country, drawing up to 10 percent of the electorate, if they have Eurocommunist politics. Or they are sects if they retain Marxist-Leninist orthodoxy. The Eurocommunists have some influence within the broader left, and the only question is why they still maintain a separate organizational existence rather than influencing the larger Social Democratic parties from within. The sects will remain without influence and are increasingly embarrassed by Soviet and Eastern European reforms, a stance that draws them closer to Cuba, Romania, and China. The exceptions are a few Mediterranean orthodox Communist parties like those of Portugal, Greece, and Cyprus. There are also some Trotskyist organizations that seem frozen in time although they often produce interesting journals. The Maoists are gone with the wind. Third Worldism (i.e., support for revolutionary movements and governments in the Third World) is quite marginal on the left as depressing tales about the performance of these regimes keep coming in. It was a political fashion that lasted for just about two decades among the student and far left. It combined a love of the exotic, a love of danger and violence, and normal guilt about the Third World.

The anarchists are enjoying a minor revival around the social movements, particularly those engaged in direct—that is, antielectoral or parliamentary—action. These are strong among squatters in West Berlin, Amsterdam, Copenhagen, and London. All these groups are a part of the European left, but the term "Euroleft" tends to be used more narrowly to refer to the broad and loose alliance of socialist and Eurocommunist groups, as well as smaller independent leftist groups and journals that tend to back mainstream left coalition governments.

The religious left is present in several forms. There are Catholic unions, particularly in Italy, as well as left wings of Social Christian parties. Neither of these is programmatically distinct from the Democratic Socialists. To be sure, the far left fringes of the Catholic left provided recruits for the Red Brigades in Italy in the early 1970s, but that was a period during which much of the unorthodox left experimented with ideas, and sometimes actions, inspired by Third World guerrillas. It remained a marginal phenomenon. The more general development in the 1970s was that Catholic unions moved broadly to the left and toward secularism. The Catholic trade union federation in France faced this problem in the 1970s and changed into a secular organization that is the closest to the Socialist party of the three labor federations in France. There are also journals inspired by the Catholic left, such as the very influential French journal *L'Esprit*. Both Protestant and Catholic activists were, and are, prominent in the peace movement as it spread beyond the traditional pacifist or peace churches. These groups, which are very numerous in West Germany and the Netherlands and to a lesser extent in Italy and Great Britain, range in politics from a general Euroleft to the more single-issue focus of the social movements. What also characterizes them is their greater sensitivity to North-South issues, campaigns against hunger and oppression in the Third World, and work with non-European migrants. The religious left is a very significant, though often overlooked, part of the Euroleft. It votes for the Democratic Socialist parties in most cases.

Then there are the social movements of the left and the right. Most writers tend to focus on the social movements on the left end of the spectrum. My own view is that the movements of the right, ranging from racists and nationalists to religious fundamentalists and nationalist populists, are more significant and numerous and will grow in both Western and Eastern Europe. So will inherently antipolitical movements, or postpolitical movements like Eastern religions and other New Age phenomena. Nevertheless I will first turn to a brief examination of the social movements of the left. They are smaller but will be significant in the immediate future because they form a part of the future majority coalitions and are a cultural phenomenon of considerable and long-range importance.

The New Social Movement on the Left

A little bit like virtue and goodness, it is taken for granted that one *knows, or should know,* what these movements are. Again, as with virtue, it is assumed that it is wrongheaded to be agnostic and ask too many coolly analytic questions about what type of forces these movements organize, and what their politics are. To put it in another way, asking analytic questions about the new social movements assumes that cold, rational analysis can be applied to them as to any other social phenomenon. Such an assumption is in itself considered by some, particularly the cultural feminists in these movements, to indicate hostility. This is because some of these movements claim that they transcend traditional "patriarchal" or "Eurocentric" or even "productivistic" logic.

In fact, radical feminists, peace activists, and ecologists place great emphasis on the difference between the "old" left "masculine" insistence on logic and argument as against the "new" social movement and feminist emphasis on intuition and faith. In that regard it is allied to a "New Age" sensibility that stresses the nonrational, the mytho-poetic and natural. "Natural" here is used in a special sense to mean in concert with nature rather than attempting to dominate it. This view is therefore hostile to the cold, rational logic of an industrial civilization.

Given the increasingly evident ecological crisis, the ever greater parts of our lives that are subject to the stresses of a social system that insists on growth for its own sake, this is not an unreasonable individual reaction. To attempt to understand and analyze, at least in my case here, is not necessarily to reject much of what these activists are trying to do. The intuitive and committed side of social criticism and socialism has to be reintroduced into the broad left culture and the social democratic movement if this movement is to survive in the long run.

Generally there is agreement that, when they do mobilize large constituencies, which is not all that often, women's, peace, and ecology movements must be included in any reasonable definition of the new social movements. Under some circumstances ethnic protest groups, immigrant groups, organized students, human rights groups, gay and lesbian groups, and even countercultural groups can also qualify. Ethnic and immigrant protest groups can assume great importance because their very existence signals the development of a more heterogeneous society and the perpetuation of discrimination and racism. Racial and ethnic issues are more fundamental than issues of political choice because they concern something as basic as personal and group identity, which in most instances is not subject to personal definition.

The same, of course, can be said of groups addressing gender oppression. Both deal with the kinds of issues that belong to what French theorists used to call the "pays réel" in contract to "pays légal," that is, "real country" defined by tradition and intense ties of kinship and custom, as opposed to the "legal country" of laws and bureaucratic, impersonal, universalist legalism. Issues affecting the "real country" are capable of generating great passion and commitment and mobilizing great numbers. This is illustrated by ethnic and national liberation movements on the "left" and by conservative populist nationalism on the right. It is also illustrated by the passion aroused by questions of gender as was shown by the referenda on divorce and the struggle over reproductive rights in Italy, Ireland, and the United States.

Direct action single and multi-issue organizations and less formally organized groups, squatters, free schools, alternative child-rearing communes and the like can also sometimes become types of social movements. Entire neighborhoods in major cities and university towns have been dominated by alternative communities and social movements. Some—West Berlin, Amsterdam, and Copenhagen, for example—have become international centers of "movement" sentiment, in much the same way that the Left Bank of Paris, London's Soho, and Greenwich Village in New York were centers of cultural rebellion in the past. A number of alternative institutions and groups are part of a libertarian and anarchist milieu that has existed on the left as long as the socialist movement has. The pre-World War I East Side in New York, and certain neighborhoods in Paris, Milan, Barcelona, and London, had dense networks of alternative free schools, communes, cultural centers, free theaters, printing shops, and noninstitutional and antiparliamentary direct action movements.

Quite often one seems to be dealing with a sensibility or mood rather than political or social issue groups or ideas, let alone movements. It seems that the social movements are sometimes found on the fringes of Bohemia and are at least as much of a cultural phenomenon as a subject of politics as usually defined. But then cultural moods and movements are definitely a part of politics, although any study of Italian society in the early 1920s will demonstrate that cultural politics are not at all necessarily associated with the left.

The wide range covered by the term "new social movements" should alert us that we are probably dealing with several very different types of issues and groups here. It is also reasonably clear that whatever else a number of these "new" social movements are, many of them are neither new nor social, and moreover a great many are not easily defined as actual movements. This does not make them necessarily less important. Just as the problem of size and outreach bedevils those who would define new social movements, so too does their practical day-to-day political orientation confuse many, very often including their adherents.

The routinization of contemporary socialism in its revolutionary Marxist form, the most widespread secular faith of our century, also has left a void—that is, the cultural and sometimes political space created by the new social movements of the left and of the right. Until the current detente, apocalyptic fears of nuclear holocaust fueled this hunger for commitment, and the movements could fill a need for many persons that neither traditional organized religion nor the mass parties of the left satisfied. How else can one explain the intense zeal of the protesters against the nuclear missiles and U.S. bases in West Germany and Britain in the early 1980s?

No serious person really expected a war in Europe or a world war. An entire movement subculture and faith developed with its own powerful language and symbolism, and these things were there not to be analyzed but, on the contrary, to be believed. What these movements often lack in numbers and impact on their societies, they often make up for with enthusiasm and faith.

Part of the confusion about the social movements of the left stems from the degree to which these overlap with a generationally specific youth culture. This was particularly the case when the student movements of the 1960s moved off campus to form the core of anti-imperialist, anti-Vietnam War, and other movements. Even at that time, sometimes on the fringes, sometimes closer to the center, culture radicalism that included experimentation with drugs and alternative life-styles was present. The youth culture in America, however, is staunchly anti-intellectual and resists any long-range engagement with complex issues. It is hostile to the whole notion that there *are* complex issues, treating such an assertion as a form of middle-age sellout. That mood leads a focus on single issues and to action or, even better, "action" such as the perennial spring mobilizations or marches, rather than organizing for alternatives to the existing structures of economic and political power and authority. The problem is that the cultural style of the young in the United States has had a massive influence for good and evil on the young in all advanced industrial societies, or perhaps more accurately on the young throughout the world.

Social Movements Based on Gender Oppression

The most significant and serious new social movements in advanced industrial societies since the student rebellions of the 1960s have been the women's, environmental, and peace movements. There are other important groups, but they lack the near-universal nature of the first three, which have emerged in all democratic industrial societies with the exception of the peace movement in France. Movements in solidarity with Third World liberation struggles and against intervention are limited to a few countries, and rival claims for support do a good deal to diffuse these.

Squatters' movements are quite important in a few large cities in specific locales. Gay and lesbian protest movements do not have broad appeal, nor are they as widespread as the women's and ecological movements. Wherever the Greens have organized, a multi-issue movement coalition is in effect formed. That inevitably leads to trouble because *movements* by nature refuse to accept that issues can be given different orders of priority. It is also probably the case that peace organizations and the peace movement will become far less significant in the near future if the detente continues. This will make women's and ecological movements even more central.

To be sure, peace groups and feminist and free cultural and educational groups are old friends of the left. They have always been there. A minimal reading of nineteenth-century and early twentieth-century socialist pamphlets by Engels, Bebel, Lafargue, Shaw, Wilde, Emma Goldman, Margaret Sanger, and Elizabeth Gurley Flynn should quickly prove the point. It is simply not true that the old official socialist movement paid no attention to either gender oppression or the social construction of the nuclear family. The two most popular pamphlets in the old socialist movement were Bebel's "The Woman Question" and George Bernard Shaw's "An Intelligent Woman's Guide to Socialism and Capitalism." Generations of Socialists were recruited with those. Generations were also somewhat miseducated with Engels's "Origins of Private Property and the Family," a pamphlet that can be fairly described as an all-out assault on the historic roots of patriarchy.[3]

Nevertheless, organized communism and social democracy preoccupied with electoral politics and real prospects of wielding power in the years after 1945 had allowed their historical concerns with gender oppression to become a matter of routine statements and legislation until the most recent revival of the women's movements. The massive revival of women's movements in the 1970s and the increased political mobilization of women, which began in the United States and rapidly spread to the Western European countries, has changed that attitude. This change involved considerable debate and conflict between independent women's organizations and groups affiliated with the Communist and Socialist parties. The political victory here clearly belongs to independent women's groups and socialist feminist activists who, in effect, transformed a number of the staid official women's organizations of the left, and thus the left itself. By the late 1980s a number of the larger Social Democratic parties, including those of Norway and West Germany, adopted a policy of assuring that a minimum of 40-50 percent of the leading posts in the party and government would be reserved for women.

Socialists and their unions in Europe have become much more sensitive to so-called women's issues (so-called because those issues are never strictly limited in impact to women but have always had an important bearing on families and thus on the young in all societies). The Swedes have probably gone the furthest in attacking gender stereotyping beginning with preschool and school training and have developed parental leave policies designed to encourage *both* parents to play a role in child rearing. Obviously this is a long-range and complex area of social and political activity and one that touches on widespread and deeply held assumptions and beliefs. Success in this area will require imagining different types of alternative arrangements that can replace the nuclear family for those who desire such options. The egalitarian societies of the future will be more varied and pluralistic than any current definition of the "normal" nuclear family can project. But people obviously should also be able to pick *that* option too, without being financially and socially locked into dependence and inequality. This will require that Socialists defend not only democracy, which is essentially a collective category, but also *individual liberty*, which is the right of people to live different lives no matter how "weird" or unreasonable these may seem, so long as they harm no one and interfere with no one else's rights. There are those vast areas of personal life that must never be permitted to become the subject of the will of the political community. This is above all true in most cases of voluntary associations where power, money, or institutional domination is not involved—for example, with regard to what consenting adults do to please each other sexually.

Not all oppressions spawn social movements, however, nor do all struggles for rights generate social movements. The struggle for civil liberties deserves support everywhere, despite the fact that, except in some instances and for a limited time under tottering authoritarian regimes, struggles for civil liberties do not always provide a basis for broad-based and lasting social movements. This clearly does not make these efforts less worthy of support, however.

On the other hand it is difficult to organize left political parties and unions today since abstract and presumably objective class identity no longer acts as the solely decisive political "signifier." It must be added that class by itself was never all that automatically linked to left politics and voting. There were always "deferential" working-class voters who voted and politically supported their "betters." It is true, however, that the bulk of the backing for the parties of the left in Western Europe for almost a century came from the industrial working class.

Moreover, the working class now includes the masses of white-collar and pink-collar workers who have become increasingly unionized and tend to vote for the left. At other points it may well be that gender or even ethnic identity will determine political affiliation; all of these factors cut across the number of roles people play in real life. While we all live a multiplicity of roles the relevant question, for political and social movements, is which situations bring to the surface which role as the salient one, as the one that will predict the behavior and attitudes of the greatest number of people. My view is that it will most often be class, now defined to include the economically insecure, heavily female, currently recomposing working class in modern industrial societies. I do not believe it will be gayness or generational grievances, although those identities can lead to major militant struggles for expanding democratic and citizens' rights. The issues of class clearly are not counterposed to a focus on social movements and the struggles for empowerment and widening democratic entitlement.

The reemergence of social movements has been of great importance in helping to re-create a broad new left not restricted to electoralism or economic demands. The old mainline socialist left was a much more varied, more pluralistic, culturally flexible, and radical movement. It was that richness which made it possible to speak of a socialist *movement* rather than only of socialist electoral parties and trade unions. That movement was a complex network of mutual aid societies, reading clubs, alternative socialist schools for children and adults, theater groups, women's groups, cooperatives, cultural organizations, sports clubs, and the like. In short, the movement was an alternative culture within the capitalist society.

One can be cynical today and point out that old left culture was not all that adversarial. Many of these institutions were instruments for upward social mobility for workers. Nevertheless this old movement culture of both the old socialist and communist left filled a genuine need. Much of what was taken care of by the autonomous organizations of the left later became services provided by the new welfare states. Those welfare states represented on one hand a victory of the old workers' movement, at the very least being a concession to avoid more radical changes or social disruption; on the other hand, something was genuinely lost when institutions of mutual aid on the left were replaced by impersonal bureaucratic services from a welfare state. At the very least what was lost was a sense of self-motivation and responsibility—in other words, the sense of power institutions of the old left gave their participants.

Today in many countries that type of cultural milieu is found around the independent left, the Green parties and the so-called alternative groups. This is clearly a segment of the left, broadly speaking. Equally clearly it challenges the existing mass Socialist parties as they now exist. Too close an identification with this left radicalism threatens the stable electoral base. On the other hand, co-opting the broader and more attractive parts of the programs of the alternative groups expands the support of the Social Democrats among educated young voters who had never been drawn in. For a host of reasons the old, almost automatic recruitment of intellectually inclined and rebellious young workers is no longer a source of new activists. For one thing, the old homogeneous working-class neighborhoods with their autonomous subcultures no longer exist. They have been destroyed by slum clearance. For another, the state provides services and schools through which the left used to recruit. Still another factor is the greater social mobility of all modern industrial societies.

Co-optation of the more relevant parts of the Greens' program and subculture by the Social Democrats did not weaken the Green parties.

The Greens did surprisingly well in the 1988 election, which returned the Social Democrats to power in Sweden. They also continue to do well in West Germany. They clearly will be fairly successful in East Germany as well, since of the larger alternative organizations, the New Forum is distinctly "greenish." But although it is a good thing for the left to develop more pluralistic organizational and political approaches in the capitalist industrial democracies, *excessive* fragmentation will make it difficult to act on more than individual issues of reform. That fragmentation is even more damaging in the newly democratizing Eastern European countries, where it is essential to develop legitimate alternative democratic authority. To move further toward social, economic, and political change, the strategic core of the left needs to be massively organized and to draw in large-scale active participation of the type we find in the "thick" social democratic political cultures like those of Sweden, Norway, Austria, and around the Italian Communist party.

Conservative Social Movements

It is not at all clear that the more numerous new social movements are found on the left or progressive end of the spectrum rather than on the right. For example, there is a huge revival of participatory, fundamentalist, grass-roots Christianity, as well as of orthodox grass-roots Judaism and Islam. These surely are of at least as much significance as some of the leftist social movements, and those who do not accept this are guilty of secular intellectual elitism. Despite the essentially secular nature of most intellectuals on the left who write about social movements, the mass of adherents of informally organized movements with a wide following are religious. To give only one example, this *nota bene* clearly applies to the largest movements among African Americans in the United States, both with regard to the traditional Christian churches and the more radically separatist Black Muslims.

Thus the secularism and general "leftism" of most analysts of social movements get in the way of a clearer view of their reality. That reality is that many significant social movements are essentially conservative, antimodern, and antidemocratic, and this can be said of the wide growth of massive, grass-roots-based populist nationalism in both Western and especially Eastern Europe and the Soviet Union. Some social movements in the Soviet Union seem to be the contemporary equivalent of the anti-Western (and thus antimodern) Russian Slavophilism of the nineteenth century. These conservative grass-roots groups quite often reflect an alienation from an impersonal, cold, noncommunitarian social order that comes with modernity and the possessive individualism characteristic of competitive capitalism. But they are also a signal that modern impersonal capitalism, or perhaps just industrial societies in general, has frayed the bonds of community and solidarity beyond tolerance for many.

Cool, modern, and decent welfare state democracies do not fill this void. They are infinitely more decent than the existing alternatives, but they cannot make up for the absence of community and faith. Something has to fill this vacuum, since humans are supremely social animals. The death of God or at least of God's organization on earth, the established church, has left for many a huge void. Such voids are often filled with enraged movements seeking a return to an idealized traditional society and values.

Conservative social movements are widespread throughout Eastern Europe and the Soviet Union. A partial explanation for this is that the Communists have systematically repressed coherent, conscious, and articulate political opposition. What they did tacitly tolerate was romanticized nationalism and xenophobia. What they explicitly tried to spread was contempt for "decadent" Western parliamentarianism, pluralism, and democracy. Some of the antidemocratic propaganda fell on historically fertile ground. In any case, parliamentary multiparty democracy and a culture of tolerance for other ideas and values could be represented as alien to the authentic national and religious traditions of most countries in the area. The organized groups were relatively easier to repress than informal networks, which maintained traditional, usually nationalist and religious values. For that matter, loose organization was an asset to left-wing social movements under dictatorships, which is why alternate movements survived while alternate parties did not.

Right-wing social movements usually mobilize around nationalist, crudely populist, xenophobic, and traditionally religious slogans and programs. Examples abound, the Serbian nationalist, so-called anti-bureaucratic revolution in Yugoslavia, the only slightly covertly xenophobic and anti-Semitic Democratic Forum in Hungary, the orthodox nationalist Pamyat in the Soviet Union, and anti-Semitic right-wing Catholic nationalism in Poland being the typical and better-known ones. The murderous rage let loose in Armenia and Azerbaijan is clearly rooted in right-wing, religiously inspired, and widely popular nationalism. It has all the characteristics of a broad, spontaneous social movement. So does the nationalism in Moldavia, Georgia, Uzbekistan, and the Baltic states, which all too often includes the frequent if uninspiring demand to oppress *their* minorities. Whatever else the remaining Basque terrorists are today, they are not democracy-loving leftists.

French-speaking Walloon and Flemish nationalist movements in Belgium, not to mention the ongoing tribal war-fare in Northern Ireland, should give pause to those who think intolerant grass-roots nationalist movements are characteristic of the less developed parts of Europe and the world. On the contrary, tolerance of differences, that most essential of all qualities for a genuinely democratic society, is rare indeed. The future of these right-wing nationalist and populist movements is therefore unfortunately at least as bright as that of democratic parties and organizations in Eastern Europe and the Soviet Union.

Years of authoritarian repression did not, unsurprisingly, give birth to an open, democratic, and tolerant political culture. Jeffersonian or even Millian democrats do not abound in those societies. Solzhenitsyn's right-wing, nationalist, and traditional politics should have been a warning. Such reaction was not the smallest historical price those countries will have to pay for a considerable time for the lost years under dull, repressive, spiritually deadening, and economically retrograde dictatorships.

One of the reasons the equivalent nationalist and populist movements are likely to remain weaker in Western Europe is the democratic space that has been won over the years by the socialist and labor movements and the new social movements of the left. Racist political movements and parties in France have created as a reaction the mass anti-racist movement *S.O.S. Racisme*, and the right-wing vote seems limited to around 10 percent. The situation in Germany and Denmark is similar. Nevertheless democracy is not a natural condition of advanced industrial societies, regardless of what theorists of the linkage of the market and democracy claim. On the contrary, it is hard-won and ever endangered terrain for individual liberty and social equity.

Progressive Social and Labor Movements Supplement Each Other

Social movements of the left and Social Democratic parties and unions sometimes seem to be working different sides of the street, to be addressing different clienteles and political publics. This impression, however, is an illusory and superficial one, since the overwhelming majority of the political public of social movements and Green parties expect to benefit from the pro-welfare state legislation introduced and defended by the Social Democrats. Even more, since most of them are workers, whether blue-, white-, or pink-collar, they expect to benefit from the political and economic muscle of the unions. Workers today can be and are increasingly both male and female in all advanced industrial societies. Therefore, for practical reasons as well as a matter of principle, the elimination of gender stereotyping in employment is one of the major goals of modern trade union and socialist politics. The survival and growth of the unions depend on reaching women voters and workers.

This should immediately alert one to the fact that what are in question are often—indeed, are almost always—overlapping categories, sometimes with multiple overlaps. Thus we can have an immigrant, lesbian, politically radical, poor worker. All those separate identities are subject to different, and if not equal, then very painful oppression and exploitations in both modern and traditional societies—modern industrial societies, not only capitalist industrial societies.

In fact, this oppression is not limited to industrial societies: some of the worst forms of oppression of women occur in traditional societies and communities, which is one more reason to change those societies radically. To treat the concerns raised by women's movements and feminists in Western Europe and the United States as a form of cultural imperialism is wrongheaded. Even the theories, and often the practices of national independence and Marxist movements of the societies of the South, are also alien "imports" from the imperialist heartland. They can therefore be attacked, and *are* attacked by religious traditionalists in those societies as European cultural hegemony. Both the ideology of anti-imperialism and the theories of imperialism can be subjected to the same criticism. These concepts are artifacts of "Western culture," and even the language used to express them is artifactual. What are at stake are human rights, which are no less basic for being sometimes stated with an American or Western European feminist or leftist cultural Eurocentric insensitivity.

Activity and activism, per se, do not develop alternate conceptions of the social order. Activism is just as sterile without theory and intellectual work, as theories and programs are without activism. Bridging this dilemma requires stable political party formations of the left that try to deal with all of the complexity and consequences of modern technology and posit alternative states in terms of the common good; such party formations are preferable to devoted, chiliastic, single-issue activists or those who reject modernity as such. These parties, however, become reduced to dull electoralism as an end unless they are surrounded by a milieu full of social movements and issue groups partially overlapping with and partially competing with the mass Socialist party. In short, the mass Socialist parties need the greenish social movements to retain their own *socialist* identities in contemporary Europe, Eastern and Western.

NOTES

1. A short bibliography would include Seweryn Bialer (ed.), *Sources of Contemporary Radicalism*, vols. 1 and 2 (Boulder: Westview, 1977); Frances Fox Piven and Richard Cloward, *The Politics of Turmoil* (New York: Pantheon, 1972); Lawrence Lader, *Power on the Left: The American Radical Movements since 1946* (New York: Norton, 1979); Maurice Isserman, *If I Had a Hammer: The Death of the Old Left and the Birth of the New Left* (New York: Basic Books, 1987); Chaim Waxman (ed.), *The End of Ideology Debate* (New York: Simon and Schuster, 1968): for the general development of the New Left and social movements. On class and social movements see Ellen Meiskins Wood, *The Retreat from Class* (London: Verso, 1986); *Socialist Register 1983* has three important articles, "Women, Class, and Family," by Dorothy Smith; "Masculine Dominance and the State," by Varda Burstyn, and "André Gorz and His Disappearing Proletariat," by Richard Hyman; and André Gortz, *Farewell to the Working Class: An Essay on Postindustrial Socialism* (Boston: South End Press, 1982). See also Nicos Poulantzas, *Political Power and Social Classes* (London: New Left Books, 1973), and Ernesto Laclau, *Politics and Ideology in Marxist Theory* (London: Verso, 1979). The intersection of class, gender, and social policy is discussed in Frances Fox Piven and Richard Cloward, *The New Class War* (New York: Pantheon, 1982); see a useful collection on class and the new working class in Pat Walker (ed.), *Between Labor and Capital*, and Michael Harrington, *The Next Left* (New York: Henry Holt, 1986), for a discussion of the issues of class and full employment. See also the wheel rediscovered in André Gorz, "S(He) Who Does Not Work Shall Eat All the Same: Tomorrow's Economy and Proposals from the Left," in *Dissent*, Spring 1987. The issues of strategy and tactics are contemporary and very controversial.

2. See Alain Touraine, *The May Movement: Revolt and Reform* (New York: Random House, 1971); Bernard Crick (ed.), *Protest and Discontent* (London: Pelican, 1970); and a reconstructed "maoissant" New Leftist, George Katsiaficas, *The Imagination of the New Left: A Global Analysis of 1988* (Boston: South End Press, 1987); on a more sober note see Erik Hobsbawn, "1968: A Retrospective," *Marxism Today*, May 1978. See also Maurice Isserman, *If I Had a Hammer*.

3. See Werner Tonnesen, *The Emancipation of Women: The Rise and Decline of the Women's Movement in German Social Democracy 1863-1933* (London: Pluto Press, 1976). Also see section 8 in Joanne Barkan, *Visions of Emancipation: The Italian Workers' Movement since 1945* (New York: Praeger, 1984). U.S. experiences are examined in Mary Jo Buhle, *Women and American Socialism, 1870-1920* (Urbana: University of Illinois Press, 1981).

Chapter 6

A New Europe:
The Implications for the World

The Political Trends of the Early 1980s Reversed

While the early 1980s represented a kind of doldrums for the Socialist parties this was only in comparison with the major successes and hopes that had developed in the 1970s. The malaise was more spiritual than organizational. The decade-long rule of Thatcher's Conservatives in Great Britain and the two most primitively conservative U.S. administrations since the 1920s were seized on by many analysts to illustrate a world trend. The trend was supposedly in the direction of free-market economies on a world scale and it was accompanied by a new paradigm: it was not capitalism that was in crisis but rather socialism. The myth of the free market was especially strong as an ideology where it was least applicable: among the intellectuals in France (which was easily the most interventionist nation in Europe), among the new middle classes coddled and even created by state protection in communist countries of Eastern Europe, and among U.S. and British business-persons, who never hesitated to run to the state for protection and loot. All three groups would probably have starved in anything resembling a free market. But then of course the whole idea was to get the lowest two-thirds of the population off demeaning dependence on the community and the state.

The world was told that what ailed the British and U.S. economies, and by implication those of other capitalist democracies, was not a backward, ideologically confrontational *management* unused to competition. Nor was the problem inadequate investment by the state in re-

97

search, transportation, housing, and the rest of a general infrastructure, or even in educational systems, which at least in Britain and the United States produce ever less well prepared candidates for the jobs that are emerging from the economic restructuring of these societies. Rather the problem was exorbitant labor costs imposed by a greedy and overpowerful labor movement, and an underclass spoiled by overgenerous and character-weakening social programs and excessive dependence on the state.

This approach sounded modern and tough and moreover had two enormously happy side effects: it justified massive cuts in taxes for the better off, which was necessary to create the illusion of scarce resources, which would in turn mandate cutting welfare programs—not out of greed and social meanness, but rather for the sake of morally and empirically sound social policy. The second effect of this new paradigm was the conclusion that the poor were responsible for their own plight, *and*, oh, happy thought, that doing anything for them would be positively harmful to the economy and above all to the poor themselves. How the new conservative policymakers in Britain and the United States worried about the poor! The most popular version of that argument in the United States is found in Charles Murray's *Losing Ground*, but the good news spread far and wide. Greed was good; cuts in social spending built character and by implication the work ethic and, by further implication, a decent society.

This trend was reinforced by a number of concurrent, not necessarily connected, phenomena. On the one hand there arose a very visible and highly publicized new school of French intellectuals (most of them former Maoists), known as the New Philosophers, which loudly announced the end of the cultural domination of the left in France—France by implication, since for French intellectuals the center of the world is Paris (just as New York and London serve this purpose for American and British philosophers), or if not the center of the world, at least its intellectual trendsetter. In any case the left was out of fashion, both in its funky but regrettably authoritarian form as Marxism-Leninism and its insufficiently exciting social democratic form. The exceptions were on the margins of power and in social movements that did not threaten to take power.

In Britain the Labour party seemed to enter a permanent downward spiral that was accompanied by a genuine programmatic crisis reinforced by a series of electoral defeats. Ironically it was the intellectuals around the Eurocommunist British Communist party who first began to draw strategic conclusions from the new development. Some of these are quite sensible and are found in *The Forward March of Labor Halted?*

(edited by Eric Hobsbawm). Throughout the 1980s in both Britain and the United States, labor and its allies were clearly in retreat as the most savage antiunion and antiwelfare campaign since the 1920s unfolded in those countries. It seemed doomed to last forever.

Whatever hopes had existed that the reformed communism of the Eurocommunists would find a new, attractive, and presumably more radical path than social democracy died a quiet and unmourned death in the 1980s. The same message was being delivered by the conservatives on one hand and the ecologists on the other. There would be no more economic growth, and as a result welfare state programs were on the defensive in the face of major new economic constraints; living standards would stagnate, if not decline. To be sure, the decline would not affect everyone but the United States would sternly curb the costs incurred by welfare mothers and their children while expanding the military budget to unprecedented heights in peacetime. In Britain the local governments and education would be savaged. Happily, for a whole set of historical reasons European countries continued to resist increases in military spending, despite pressure from the United States, and maintained their welfare states more or less intact. Europeans quite simply seem to expect considerably more services from their governments. The myth of the self-reliant cowboy who treats the state as a hostile impediment to his right to do his own thing is quite properly relegated to the screen and to the underdeveloped regions of southern Italy and Sicily. Elsewhere in Europe the state is viewed not as the enemy but as a purveyor of necessary services in a modern economy and society.

Social Democratic Revival within the EEC

What few people noticed was that the broad left vote remained relatively constant and that almost every opinion poll in every imaginable advanced industrial society showed that welfare state programs remained widely popular. This proved to be the case even in the United States, where such programs are popular, particularly when they are universal; it's just that taxes are not. In other words, the population at large, just like the business community, would like to get something for nothing. The Socialists remained the clearly dominant part of the left in every single Western European country (with the oddball exception of Italy, where the Communist party is the largest party, and which, as was noted earlier, is entering the Socialist International and is really therefore not an exception), and the left retained its plurality within the European Parliament.

In the meantime while preoccupied with winning elections as usual, the larger Social Democratic parties were also busily overhauling their programs and expanding their appeal to new social groups. After all, there is only so much you can do with a sheer celebration of the socially desirable effects of *greed* as a program, and Thatcherism and Reaganism did not seem to go much beyond greed. Like cold baths for soft young people greed was supposed to be bracing for societies gone soft by coddling the undeserving poor.

The current debate within the largest and most significant Social Democratic party in the world, the German SPD, represents a promising new departure. It points to a major historical theoretical and strategic shift that is just as significant as the Keynesian reformist program adopted in 1959 at Bad Godesberg. The new direction has been heavily influenced by three relatively recent political and social factors. The first is the collapse of the belief in the ability of Keynesian economic management to provide full employment and an expanding welfare state *without* having to face the politically difficult issue of income redistribution. The second factor is major openings toward Eastern Europe and the Soviet Union as they begin democratic reforms that make possible the end of the cold war and of the political and military dependence on the United States. The last factor (but certainly not the least) is the growing influence of the Greens and alternative parties and social movements, especially the women's and peace movements, representing significant publics that the Social Democrats must reach if broad left-wing majorities are to be possible.

In summary, the new thinking in the German Social Democratic party calls for an ecologically responsible, low-energy, socially sensitive strategy for full employment and greater egalitarianism. It also proposes a broadened strategy of economic opening toward the "East" and a continued consolidation of the European Community, which is to be pushed into major initiatives to deal with the widening North/South gap along the lines of the Brandt-Manley proposals. Combined, these initiatives necessarily spell out a policy of greater Western European assertiveness in dealing with its traditional alliance with the United States. Given the huge resources the German Social Democrats have at their disposal it is safe to assume that this new "German" line, supported by the Italian CP and the Scandinavian parties, will be dominant in European socialism in the 1990s. German unification can only increase the influence of this viewpoint, which has the virtue of appealing to the electorates politicized by the social movements while retaining much of the old blue-collar voting base of social democracy. It is also sufficiently moderate and broad in its class appeal to allow the type of consensual government that is widely accepted as legitimate. European Socialists today are firmly committed both to the defense and extension of democracy and to individual liberty. Production of goods, however, is not a personal activity but a supremely social task.

Therefore the long-range goal of a socialist policy is that production should be democratically controlled and organized with whatever plurality of forms of social and private property and combinations of market (allocation by plan that is both indirect and a more deliberate coordination) turns out to be most consistently effective. Moving beyond the welfare state requires genuine democracy and popular power, which in turn implies, no matter how unfashionable it may now be, the massive transfer of private control by the capitalist minorities over the economic and financial system to democratic social control.

Despite, or rather *because* of, negative experiences with centrally run and bureaucratically planned economies in Communist party-run states, it is unavoidable that democratic social control over the economy and the financial system also includes the use of a democratically controlled state, with a popularly determined and responsible administration. No amount of insistence on workers' control and self-management, which will be introduced widely in any socialist-run society, can eliminate the role of democratic planning by the state.

The experiences of the first French socialist government in the early 1980s suggest that there are limits to what is possible for autarkic experiments with the economy of a single state. Conversely, the experiences of Austria, Sweden, Switzerland, and Japan demonstrate that single countries do have a substantial range of options in resisting general economic trends and that this ability is not based on the existence of socialist or nonsocialist governments. This suggests a common ground between "statist" (i.e., interventionist) Eurocrats and Socialist and Labor parties within the EEC concerning policies that should be anything but unplanned and left to the tender mercies of the market.

To maintain full employment and a welfare state in a period of world economic stagnation and in the teeth of the hostility of the international banking system, what is essential is a government that is *interventionist* in the economy. This requires neither central planning nor government ownership of the commanding heights of the economy. What it does require is the political will to have an industrial and social policy. Persistent attacks on the concept of full employment of the social democratic labor movements by some academic leftists are quite puzzling. Essentially the argument appears to be that it is important at this stage in history to separate the right to an income from the obligation to work. This is either banal, since in practice it is accepted by the most orthodox of European Social Democrats who reject "workfare" and the notion that people have to be driven to work by fear, or it is a distortion of what the call for full employment, or its closest possible equivalent under capitalism, has historically meant in the labor movement. For the socialist movement and its labor unions it has always meant the creation of decent, well-paid, socially useful jobs. There is a "postmodern" argument against full employment that was also voiced in the old socialist movement. Paul Lafargue, Marx's son-in-law, even wrote a pamphlet entitled "Why Work?" A more contemporary argument is found in John Keane's "Work and the Civilizing Process" in his *Democracy and Civil Society*. I am uncomfortable with this argument and believe it to be wrong, since a new civilization will be based not merely on new ways of distributing goods but *also and centrally* on the reorganization and democratization of production.

The more economically integrated European Community provides both a larger arena and natural transnational alliances within which to carry out social policies that are not based on the ethics of a social Darwinist jungle. The idea that social misery and unemployment are natural forces that are impervious to social policy will be remembered as an interesting superstition of "Anglo-Saxon" political elites and their intellectual courtiers.

Common agreement on *industrial and social* policy does not assume agreement on much beyond the desirability of maintaining relatively high employment and sufficient minimal common social policies to make the conditions of doing business within a unified European "space" (i.e., the EEC and EFTA combined) relatively similar. On this both labor and capital within Europe can very generally agree. Capitalist elites, when accustomed to neocorporatist arrangements as the ones in Continental Europe are, *prefer* to have health, job training and retraining, and pensions taken care of by the society as a whole rather than by individual enterprise. Unions do not like to compete for labor costs with low-wage labor, which is further unprotected by social legislation. Employers, particularly when movement of capital is subject to some controls, prefer to compete under conditions where their rivals do not have much lower labor costs *and* full unlimited access to their markets.

One of the most obvious reasons for the weakness of labor in the United States, for example, is the huge unorganized labor market in the South. European labor will try to avoid such pitfalls by gradually equalizing wages and conditions as much as possible. This is true not only of Mediterranean members of the EEC, it especially applies to Eastern Europe nations. It is reasonable of Eastern European labor to expect massive help from Western European unions in setting up genuine and militant trade unions and developing prolabor legislation where it is not already on the books. That is not only a matter of solidarity; it is also a question of economic survival for the highly paid union labor sectors of the Western European economy. Therefore Western European labor and the Social Democratic parties will be politically *interventionist* and internationally minded rather than isolationist.

From Trans-European to International Policies and Strategies

Some of the international policies developed to serve a unified Europe will represent a broad transclass and suprapolitical consensus; others will be specific to the labor movement or the financial and industrial elites of Europe, just like the situation *inside* the EEC and the wider "space" in Europe. Inside the EEC there will be continual tension between those who regard welfare state legislation as representing a "done deal," as the outer limit of social legislation.

The defense and imaginative and intelligent expansion of the welfare state are not minor issues. For one thing it is clearly the most broadly popular and publicly accepted part of the current socialist programs. It directly affects the lives of millions who are alive today and creates the social and political terrain on which policies and strategies for going further can be developed. Socialists therefore insist that the social welfare state as a principle of organization of modern industrial capitalist democracies is a part of the democratic social contract, a civic right, not a field for political bargaining. In a modern democracy an attack on the welfare state is an attack on the legitimacy of the social order itself.

An advanced welfare state will be increasingly egalitarian. The most effective way to advance egalitarianism without stifling initiative is continually to reduce economic and social differences through a combination of progressive taxes and massive investments in universally available and distributed social goods — schools, child care, health, culture, housing, leisure, pensions, and the rest — thus sharply reducing the part of income that takes the form of salaries. European unification makes it essential that certain minimal parameters of social democratic social policies be enacted among all European nations. There are many reasons for this, not the least of which concern questions of morality and principle. However, while morality and principle must be the backbone of any contemporary democratic socialist politics, there are practical reasons why egalitarian social policies and a network of social services must be implemented across the Continent. For one thing it will not do within the protected European market to have large islands of cheap unprotected labor. This would unfairly benefit such areas in attracting investments, although far more than cheap labor is needed to attract investments, as I argued in chapter 3. In fact, it is the areas with the highest wages and the most secure labor movements that attract the most investments in the European Community. Capital is not pouring into the Mediterranean regions or into Portugal and Ireland. Nevertheless, extensive income differences within Europe would also create unhealthy pressures for migration, which in turn harms the country from which the migrants come, as entire cohorts of young men and women abandon communities, returning to them only in old age and for vacations. Massive migration also creates major difficulties for the host countries, including housing shortages and a host of social problems that are easily avoidable.

While free migration must remain a cornerstone of decent democratic policy within a unified Europe, it remains desirable for communities to continue existing within their own authentic cultural settings. What this means is that while migration must remain free, economic pressures that force millions of young women and men to emigrate must be eliminated or at least sharply reduced. It may be utopian to think this can be done on a worldwide scale in the foreseeable future, but it is not at all utopian to believe this is possible within a unified Europe.

Welfare states combined with parliamentary democracy provide the optimal terrain on which to push for social changes that would lead to a transformation into something which could be called democratic socialism—that is, a considerably more egalitarian society, with wide elements of industrial democracy (including workers' control), genuine community participation and power over the state services and bureaucracies, and increasing and imaginative use of free time to enrich individual lives and participation in the society and economy. One hardwon lesson from the past decades is that such a society cannot replace but must incorporate the present forms of parliamentary democracy and political contestation. The other equally important lesson should make social movements and political parties of the left deeply suspicious of all *totalizing* programs, all programs which insist that party politics must be at the center of each individual's existence.

There are powerful arguments for a radical assault on the organization of work in modern industrial society. The huge increases in productivity and breakthroughs in productive technology of the past three decades have been inequitably distributed. Within advanced industrial societies the rich have gotten richer and workers have become much more insecure. They have had to bear the lion's share of the cost of the shift from smokestack to postindustrial organization of work. A radical cut in the workday, workweek, and worklife of people can be financed by a frankly redistributionist wealth tax, rather than in income tax increases that hit middle and lower income groups. Technological increases in productivity now make the traditional organization of work irrational and antisocial, since it forces millions onto the scrap heap of unemployment even though the economic capacities exist to redistribute work and income more justly. It is also unfair in that it remains essentially top-down and authoritarian. Changes in the character of the work force, as well as in the nature of work, make the old demand for self-management or workers' control both rational and possible. Unfortunately the past societywide experiment with self-management in Yugoslavia does not provide much of an argument either way, since it occurred within a society in which the Communist party has retained its monopoly on power in the state and the economy. Clearly the idea of democracy in the workplace combined poorly with an authoritarian political system. The reverse is also true: a genuinely democratic political culture cannot stop at the door of one's place of work.

For a radical assault on the hours, days, and years of work to be anything but sheer economic suicide, the labor movement and its allies must make that push internationally. The logical place to begin is within a unified European "economic space" combining the EEC and EFTA, which will be in place in 1992. Sheer self-preservation will lead to an extension of minimal European labor standards to Eastern Europe beginning with East Germany and pushing similar changes at least in more advanced industrial countries for a start. Much more direct aid to unions in the newly industrialized countries like Brazil, South Korea, Malaysia, and Taiwan will be needed from the labor movements in the advanced industrial world. Given the relations of strength that means, practically speaking, the European labor movement in most cases. Given the ability of multinationals to shift funds and production around the world, the reasons for the internationalization of labor strategy are obvious. That is one more reason why even moderate reformist labor-based parties must now put the question of control over the export of capital and jobs on the political agenda. The only way to keep this issue from becoming a breeding ground for xenophobia and nationalism is to make it an issue of international labor solidarity, that is, to help the weaker labor movements in Eastern Europe and the Third World.

The international distribution of the results of technological breakthroughs has been unjust. Much of the Third World is poorer today than it was in the 1950s, despite the green revolutions and national independence. The world debt burden has made the poor countries overall *exporters* of capital. Minimal social justice is the only thing that will make peace possible. Otherwise the end of the cold war will be only a backdrop for ever more desperate conflicts in a hungry South. These conflicts will tend to pull in the superpowers or at the very least to cause continual turmoil. It would be simply wrong and, embarrassing though it sometimes is to use the word, immoral to accept a world order based on the gross inequality and growing misery of what Michael Harrington rightly calls the vast majority. Such a world system cannot and should not endure.

A further argument for a redistributive strategy that is gender-sensitive and not nationally focused is that a society and therefore an economy must have a *universal* purpose and a moral justification. International economic arrangements that simultaneously doom a growing proportion of the population to marginal and insecure employment and yield greater wealth to a small minority in what is increasingly a "casino economy" cannot be it. Traditional industrial capitalism sought moral and societal justification in the assumption that the wholesale pursuit of individually and rationally selfish economic goals would produce social good, and an advanced technology and economy, which in turn would improve the lives of all. This breathtakingly utopian notion was loaded with more economic determinism than any but the most narrowly dogmatic Marxists had ever professed, and it is increasingly made a mockery of by an economy in which billions of dollars are made not by manufacturing or inventing new processes, but by moving paper and speculating on real estate.

It is in the moral critique of capitalism and market fetishism that contemporary Democratic Socialists join with the Catholic church in its statements on the economy and the dignity of labor. Fulfilling, well-paid, socially useful, and respected work is a human right superior to that of the right of capital to make larger profits. When a society cannot provide such work it is obliged at least to furnish decent, nonhumiliating support for however long it takes to restructure the economy to bring about the closest equivalent to full employment possible. Reorganizing work and an increased sensitivity to the overwhelming problems of environment on the only planet we inhabit require a new internationalism. It is a matter of self-preservation, and the European Community is more likely to move on this than either Japan or the United States for reasons having to do with both the greater willingness of Europeans to accept the regulation of corporate behavior and the more extensive organizational support there for environmental policies.

Pollution is a classic example of a problem that requires a trans-national solution as recent ecological crises in the North Sea, the Adriatic, with acid rain, and of course the Chernobyl nuclear disaster show. The greenhouse effect, which is raising the world's temperature, surely calls for an international solution. There is a need for a universalist vision of the common good and a moral drive, since human beings are not merely economic animals. There is a dimension of need and identity and a moral vision that religions at their best do provide and to which contemporary labor movements are all too often blind. However, if the Socialist parties are not to be totalizing parties, they should not try to be the substitute for religious commitment. The socialist movement should be a much broader category and provide a stronger moral thrust than do religions at their best.

The Impact of European Unity on the World

The most important impact of the unification of Europe will be on the relative position of the two superpowers. Let me be more specific. Although European unification is obviously a *process*, at each point of this process there will be naysayers who insist that what has taken place is the sum total of what will be. Nonetheless unification will slowly but surely unravel the postwar settlements as well as the structures and relationships that have developed as a result of the four decades of the cold war. Already by the end of 1989 it is clear that it will be neither limited spatially to the EEC nor to being a mere free-trade zone, although either of these would have been a significant step by itself.

Geographically it is already clear that the EFTA is joining in to create what is called the common European space. East Germany is de facto already half in and will get even further in regardless of relations between the two Germanys. Moreover the new democratizing regimes in Eastern Europe are pounding at the door and will be given at least some type of associate status. So it is Europe that is uniting and not *Western* Europe. The condition for that unification and what makes it inevitable is the end of the cold war. The content of the Europe that emerges will be far more social than those who favor a "little" Europe envision in their nightmares and of course less social than passionate Pan-Europeanists dream about. But there will be a social Europe, and Mitterrand, as the president of the EEC for the year, has wisely conceded on details but has been adamant about structure. The pot can always be improved on later. This is an old principle in collective bargaining: get a modest pension or health plan into the contract and then improve on it. So Europe will be increasingly social and will transcend old cold war divisions.

By the same token the unification of Germany is a certainty. It is possible that for years the fictional existence of two Germanys will continue to satisfy the sensibilities of the superpowers and the four occupying powers. Nevertheless the Germanys will unite, on a confederal basis, combining various institutions and services step by step until the separate states remain empty formal husks. This will occur because the vast majority of the German people want it to occur and will express that desire as soon as they are given the chance to do so democratically. It is outrageous that there are people who claim to love democracy who would block this unity in the name of the old rotten game of balance of power and maintenance of the status quo. On the other hand it is quite reasonable and legitimate to ask for guarantees that the industrial giant of unified Europe not be a military giant as well. It is thus wrongheaded and perverse to attempt to keep West Germany in NATO. On the contrary, the best guarantee for peace and stability in a unified Europe is a neutralized and demilitarized Germany—a larger Austria or, more formally, two Austrias.

A unified and demilitarized Germany inside a unified Europe! This is the stuff of dreams, and potential nightmares. Whatever else, it means a radical change in the relationship of Europe toward the superpowers. The Soviet Union appears as a petitioner for credits, aid, and increasingly for a political relationship with a common European home—that is, a common European cultural tradition and past. Let us not forget that the Soviet Union is also a part of Europe, and a recurring theme in Russian history is its need to be recognized as such. It is this need that united generations of reformers, from modernizing autocratic Czars to the democratic Decembrist rebels to the advocates of democratic reforms in the Soviet Union today. It is a matter of greatest urgency to support these reformers, to give the economic and political reforms in the Soviet Union a chance to succeed against heavy odds. Surely some sense of urgency can be communicated to make clear that the *security* of Europe and for that matter of the United States can be best assured by plowing some of the peace dividend, the immense savings that will be possible through military budget cuts, into helping the democratizing regimes in Eastern Europe and the Soviet Union. That aid will make a greater difference if it comes sooner than later, and without demeaning conditions. But of course that aid cannot really help unless fundamental political reforms free the economy from the power monopoly of the Communist party and its *nomenklatura*. Only then can economic and social reforms begin to make sense. This in turn means that extensive formal and informal contacts with the Eastern European democratic reformers, new trade unionists, managers, and intellectuals are needed. This provides a rare chance for the democratic transformation of a whole section of the world to succeed.

The discussion of what democratization must entail in Eastern Europe and the Soviet Union irrevocably opens a Pandora's box of issues. If genuinely free elections, lack of political pressure and terror, and independent trade unions are the prescription for the Eastern Europeans, why not for Central American nations and other dependencies of the United States? If manipulated elections through the monopoly of media are not really free there, how can they be free in the United States? If it is improper for governments to represent only a minority of the electorate, if broad support is needed for democratic legitimacy, what are we to say about the archaic and undemocratic electoral system in Great Britain, the first-past-the-post system that allows a minority to claim a landslide? How about the parallels between the *nomenklatura's* continued undemocratic domination in Soviet and Eastern European politics and economy and the totally undemocratic power hierarchy in the U.S. economy, not to mention the fact that over 90 percent of congressional representatives are incumbents?

A comprehensive debate about the genuine preconditions for democracy might turn out to be as bracing in some of the democracies of the West as it is in the old communist bloc. A sign of sensitivity about this issue, about the inadequacies of Western democracy, about its unfinished nature, would give more weight to discussions with Eastern European and Soviet reformers. Or is democracy only something, like free and militant unions and social protest groups, that the West will support under communism? Just how much hypocrisy will be associated with the calls for radical democratic reforms in the Soviet Union?

Massive aid to the Soviet and Eastern European economies is essential if democratic reforms are to succeed. It is clear that the United States is expressing nowhere near the sense of urgency necessary to generate sufficient aid to give democracy a fair chance in those countries. It is scandalous when compared with the unresisting way the media and Congress went along with the massive arms buildup under the Reagan administration. This is not only a scandal, it is stupid security politics. Nothing will ensure that the end of the cold war between the super powers leads to a stable international environment as much as generous and timely aid. It will not be forthcoming from the United States unless there is massive pressure from Congress. Western Europe, on the other hand, has already placed on the table economic resources that are many times over more generous. This will be reflected in political influence and cooperation as well. For that matter it will have a major effect on just which countries have long-range access to Soviet markets and resources. A unified Europe will loom increasingly large as the relevant trade, cultural exchange, and political partner for the former Communist-dominated regimes in Eastern Europe and the Soviet Union.

It is the case that economic aid cannot be properly used without thoroughgoing political reforms that force the Communist party and above all its *nomenklatura* to relinquish its stranglehold on the political and economic institutions of the Soviet Union and Eastern Europe. These reforms, however, cannot be presented as a way of crippling the rival bloc, as a just and overdue punishment. This is where the United States finds itself in a bind. Does it support democratization (including militant and free trade unions) because it is a good thing, or because it weakens an adversary? Just how much enthusiasm would there be in the White House for an American (South, Central, or North) Lech Walesa and Solidarity? This hypocrisy gap does not pass unnoticed, and this is why European labor movements and Social Democrats will have a more effective political input into the debates that develop in previous communist dictatorships. As a result, U.S. influence will decline in that region.

The role of the United States as a superpower is subject to further erosion in the Third World. Most Americans are not aware that Sweden, France, West Germany, Norway, and Holland all give considerably greater shares of their per capita national incomes for foreign aid. They do so for the usual mix of altruism and self-interest that accompanies aid. But the motive *is* different from that of the United States. The recipients are different too. The aid goes to far fewer right-wing military dictators, and there are far fewer political strings attached. The result is that Western Europe carries less political baggage in the Third World.

It is not always in a country's interest to be a superpower. Perhaps a United States in a post-cold war world will become less preoccupied with being the world policeman, with being the status quo power throughout the Third World, and will turn to concerns more befitting the most powerful democracy in the world. That could begin with turning to the long-ignored agenda of social and political reforms at home. It could do worse than to ask the question of what is the appropriate foreign and defense policy for a democratic superpower that faces no serious threat. That in turn might well lead to an international policy of the United States of which its citizens could be proud. Thus the democratic transformation in Eastern Europe and the Soviet Union and the end of the cold war will give the United States another chance in the only world we share.

Bibliography

Bibliography

Abendroth, Wolfgang. *A History of the European Working Class Movements*. New York: Monthly Review Press, 1966.

Aronowitz, Stanley. *Working Class Hero: A New Strategy for Labor*. New York: Adams Press, 1983.

Barkan, Joanne. *Visions of Emancipation: The Italian Workers Movement since 1945*. New York: Praeger, 1984.

Bialer, Seweryn, ed. *The Domestic Context of Soviet Foreign Policy*. Boulder: Westview, 1981.

Bialer, Seweryn, ed. *Sources of Contemporary Radicalism*. 2 vols. Boulder: Westview, 1977.

Boggs, Carl, and David Poltke, eds. *The Politics of Euro-Communism*. Boston: South End Press, 1980.

Bracken, Paul. *The Command and Control of Nuclear Forces*. New Haven: Yale University Press, 1983.

Brandt, Willy, and Michael Manley. *Global Challenge*. London: Pan Books, 1985.

Buhle, Mary Jo. *Women and American Socialism, 1870-1920*. Urbana: University of Illinois Press, 1981.

Carr, John. *Helmut Schmidt: Helmsman of Germany*. London: Weidenfeld and Nicolson, 1985.

Calleo, David. *Europe and America: The Future of the Western Alliance*. New York: Basic Books, 1987.

Childs, Marquis. *Sweden: The Middle Way on Trial*. New Haven: Yale University Press, 1980.

Claudin, Fernando. *The Communist Movement: From the Comintern to the Cominform*. 2 vols. New York: Monthly Review Press, 1975.

Cohen, Stephen F., and Robert C. Tucker, eds. *The Great Purge Trial*. New York: Grosset and Dunlap, 1965.

Connor, Walter D. *Socialism, Politics, and Equality*. New York: Columbia University Press, 1979.

Crick, Bernard, ed. *Protest and Discontent*. London: Pelican, 1970.

Dahl, Robert, ed. *Political Oppositions in Western Democracies*. New Haven: Yale University Press, 1966.

Dahrendorf, Ralf. *Society and Democracy in Germany*. London: Weidenfeld and Nicolson, 1960.

Debray, Regis. *Les Empires contre L'Europe.* Paris: Gallimard, 1985.

Denitch, Bogdan. *Democratic Socialism: The Mass Left in Advanced Industrial Societies.* Montclair: Allenheld and Osmun, 1981.

Denitch, Bogdan. *Limits and Possibilities: The Crisis of Yugoslav Socialism and State Socialist Systems.* Minneapolis: University of Minnesota Press, 1990.

Denitch, Bogdan. *The Socialist Debate: Beyond Red and Green.* London: Pluto Press, 1990.

Deutscher, Isaac. *The Prophet Armed.* New York: Oxford University Press, 1954.

Deutscher, Isaac. *The Prophet Disarmed.* New York: Oxford University Press, 1954.

Emmanuel, Arghiri. *Unequal Exchange.* New York: Monthly Review Press, 1972.

English, Deirdre, et al. "The Impasse of Socialist Feminism," *Socialist Review,* no. 79 (Jan.-Feb. 1985).

Feher, Ferenc, and Agnes Heller. *Eastern Left, Western Left.* Atlantic Highlands, N.J.: Humanities Press, 1987.

Gati, Charles, and Jan Triska, eds. *Blue Collar Workers in Eastern Europe.* London: Allen and Unwin, 1981.

Gorz, André. *Farewell to the Working Class: An Essay on Postindustrial Socialism.* Boston: South End Press, 1982.

Graf, William. *The German Left since 1945: Socialism and Social Democracy in the German Federal Republic.* New York: Cambridge University Press, 1976.

Harrington, Michael. *The Next Left.* New York: Henry Holt, 1986.

Harrington, Michael. *The Politics at God's Funeral.* New York: Henry Holt, 1979.

Harrington, Michael. *Socialism: Past and Future.* New York: Arcade, 1989.

Harrington, Michael. *The Twilight of Capitalism.* New York: Simon and Schuster, 1976.

Harrington, Michael. *The Vast Majority.* New York: Simon and Schuster, 1977.

Hobsbawm, Eric. "1968: A Retrospective." *Marxism Today,* May 1978.

Hobsbawm, Eric. *The Forward March of Labor Halted?* London: Verso, 1981.

Holland, Stuart. *Out of Crisis: A Project for European Recovery.* Nottingham: Spokesman Books, 1983.

Horvat, Branko. *The Political Economy of Socialism.* Armonk, N.Y.: M. E. Sharpe, 1982.

Isserman, Maurice. *If I Had a Hammer: The Death of the Old Left and the Birth of the New Left.* New York: Basic Books, 1987.

Johnstone, Diane. *The Politics of Euromissiles.* New York: Schocken Books, 1985.

Katsiaficas, George. *The Imagination of the New Left: A Global Anaysis of 1968.* Boston: South End Press, 1987.

Keane, John. *Civil Society and the State.* London: Verso, 1988.

Keane, John. *Democracy and Civil Society.* London: Verso, 1988.

Kennan, George. *Russia and the West under Lenin and Stalin.* Boston: Little, Brown, 1960.

Kennedy, Paul. *Rise and Fall of the Great Powers: Economic Change and Military Conflicts 1500-2000.* New York: Random House, 1987.

Kolakowski, Lezek. *The Main Currents of Marxism.* 3 vols. New York: Oxford University Press, 1981.

Laclau, Ernesto, and Chantal Mouffe. *Hegemony and Socialist Strategy.* London: Verso, 1985.

Laclau, Ernesto. *Politics and Ideology in Marxist Theory.* London: Verso, 1979.

Lader, Lawrence. *Power on the Left: American Radical Movements since 1946.* New York: Norton, 1979.

Lehmbruch, Gerhard, and Phillipe Schmitter, eds. *Trends towards Corporatist Intermediation.* Beverly Hills: Sage, 1979.

Mandel, Ernest. *Europe versus America.* London: New Left Books, 1968.

Mandel, Ernest. *From Stalinism to Eurocommunism.* London: New Left Books, 1979.

Meidner, R. *Employee Investment Funds.* London: Allen and Unwin, 1978.

Mittleman, James. *Out from Underdevelopment.* New York: St. Martin's Press, 1988.

Murray, Charles. *Losing Ground.* New York: Basic Books, 1984.

Piven, Frances Fox, and Richard Cloward. *The New Class War.* New York: Pantheon, 1982.

Piven, Frances Fox, and Richard Cloward. *The Politics of Turmoil.* New York: Pantheon, 1972.

Poulantzas, Nicos. *Political Power and Social Classes.* London: New Left Books, 1973.

Radice, Giles, and Lisane Radice. *Socialists in the Recession.* London: Macmillan, 1986.

Rakovski, Mark. *Towards an East European Marxism.* New York: St. Martin's Press, 1978.

Rowbotham, Sheila, et al. *Beyond the Fragment: Feminism and the Making of Socialism.* London: Merlin Press, 1979.

Snitow, Ann, et al. *The Powers of Desire.* New York: Monthly Review Press, 1983.

Stevens, John. *The Transition from Capitalism to Socialism.* London: Macmillan, 1979.

Stojanović, Svetozar. *Between Ideals and Reality: A Critique of Socialism and Its Future.* New York: Oxford University Press. 1973.

Sweezy, Paul. *Post Revolutionary Society.* New York: Monthly Review Press, 1976.

Thompson, E. P. *The Heavy Dancers.* New York: Pantheon Press, 1985.

Tilford, Richard, ed. *The Ostpolitik and Political Change in Germany.* London: Saxon House, 1975.

Tonnesen, Werner. *The Emancipation of Women: The Rise and Decline of the Women's Movement in German Social Democracy 1863-1933.* London: Pluto Press, 1976.

Touraine, Alain. *The May Movement: Revolt and Reform.* New York: Random House, 1971.

Van Pilj, Kees. *The Making of an Atlantic Ruling Class.* London: Verso, 1984.

Walker, Pat, ed. *Between Labor and Capital.* Boston: South End Press, 1979.

Waxman, Chaim, ed. *The End of Ideology Debate.* New York: Simon and Schuster, 1968.

West, Cornel. *Prophecy and Deliverance: Afro-American Revolutionary Christianity.* New York: Westminster Press, 1982.

Wood, Ellen Meiskins. *The Retreat from Class.* London: Verso, 1986.

Index

Index

Abortion: and democracy, xiv
Afghanistan, 22, 35, 58
AFL-CIO: and end of cold war, 79
Aid: to new democracies, x, xi, 13, 17, 24, 26-27, 29, 108, 109; to Third World, 13
Albania, 38, 48
Allende, Salvador, 68
Anarchists: European revival of, 84
Angola, 16
Austria, 12, 25, 33, 36, 38, 41, 43, 92, 101, 108; as role model, xii, 40, 76, 78
Austrian Peace Treaty, 32-33

Bangladesh, 42
Bebel, August, 88, 89
Belgium, 43, 44, 76, 94
Bismarck, Otto von, 70
Brandt, Willy, 71, 73, 100; *Ostpolitik* of, 39-40
Brazil, 105
Brezhnev Doctrine, 32
Bulgaria, xiii, xiv, 32, 51, 56; nationalism in, xv
Bush, George: administration of, xi, xvi, 25, 62, 66; and Panama invasion, xvii, 22-23, 29n
Butkovsky (Soviet dissident), 59

Cambodia, xvi, 7, 16, 23

Canada, 37
Capitalism: crisis in, 69; moral critique of, 106; with state intervention, 49; and Third World, 58; of welfare state, 19, 72, 77-78; and world economy, 3. *See also* Economy
Carter, Jimmy: U.S. administration of, 34, 57
Castro, Fidel, 3, 58
Catholicism: vs. capitalism and socialism, 70; socialist alliance with, 13-14, 106; unions of, 84
Ceauşescu, Nicolae, xiv
Cheney, Dick, 20
Chile, 68
China, xvi, 84
Cold war: aid to unions during, 71; ending of, ix, x, xi, 3, 13, 15, 25, 34, 45, 56, 62, 79, 100; and European division, xvi; and free market, xii; lost by authoritarian socialism, 19; stability of, 32. *See also* Soviet Union, United States
Communism: authoritarian, 69; collapse of, xiv, 3
Communist Information Bureau (Cominform). *See* Social democracy, use of term
Communist International. *See* Social democracy, use of term

119

Bogdan D. Denitch has been a professor of political sociology at the City University of New York Graduate School and Queens College since 1973. He has also taught as a visiting professor in Bologna, Paris, London, and Zagreb. Denitch is author of several books, including *Limits and Possibilities: The Crisis of Yugoslav Socialism and State Socialist Systems* (Minnesota, 1990), *The Socialist Debate: Beyond Red and Green* (1990), *Democratic Socialism* (1981), and *Legitimation of Regimes* (1979). He also contributes to *Dissent, Social Text, Telos, Politics and Society, Praxis International,* and numerous Yugoslavian journals.